STORIES OF THE NORTH CORNISH COAST

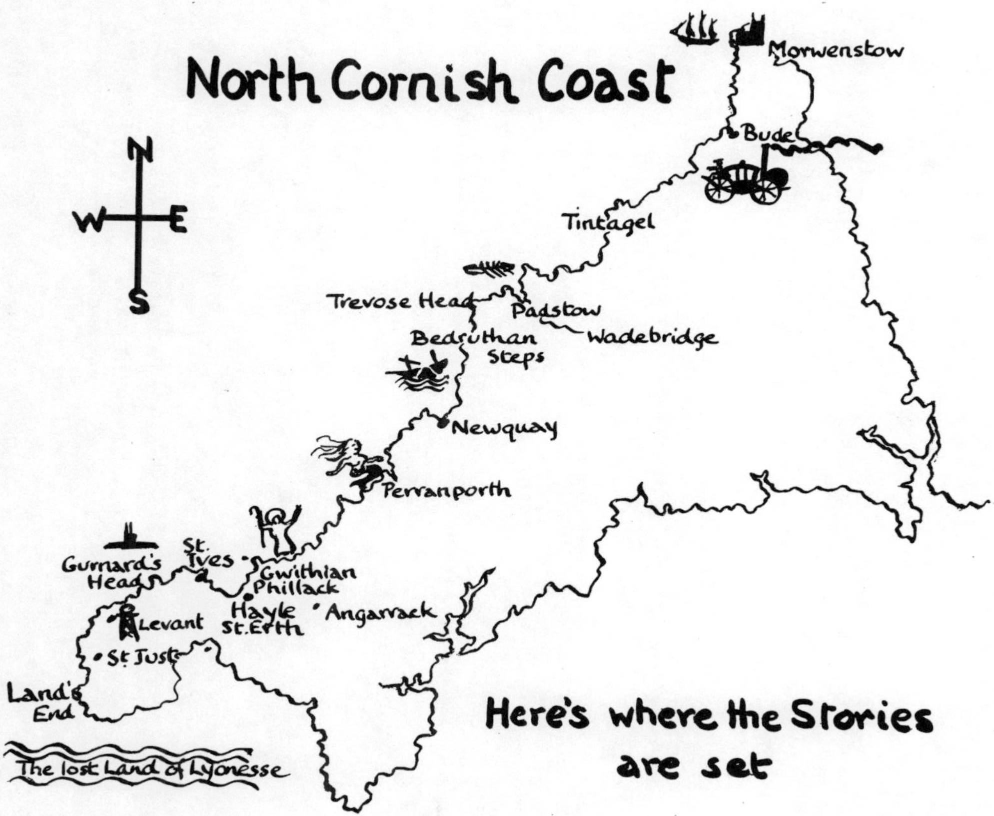
North Cornish Coast
N
W
E
S
Morwenstow
Bude
Tintagel
Trevose Head
Padstow
Wadebridge
Bedruthan
Steps
Newquay
Perranporth
St.
Ives
Gwithian
Phillack
Hayle
St. Erth
Angarrack
Gurnard's
Head
Levant
St Just
Land's
End
The lost Land of Lyonesse
Here's where the Stories
are set

Stories of the North Cornish Coast

Donald Bray

TRURAN

Published by
Dyllansow Truran, Trewolsta, Trewirgie, Redruth, Kernow.

Typeset by Helston Printers, 12 Wendron Street, Helston, Cornwall.
Printed by Penryn Litho, Antron Hill, Mabe, Penryn, Cornwall.

ISBN 0 907566 73 1

DEDICATED WITH GRATITUDE AND ALL MY LOVE
TO MY WIFE LENA

STORIES OF THE NORTH CORNISH COAST

by
Donald Bray

Stories and histories of the South Cornish Coast are told in the next book.

LIST OF ILLUSTRATIONS

PREFACE

If you cannot believe all these stories of the North Coast of Cornwall, at any rate people once thought them true, however they may have been embellished by time and much telling. They are history and biography, where I have tried to ensure that you have no doubts at all; newspaper reporting on which you may rely (except, perhaps, in its treatment of mermaids!) and legend and hearsay culled from a variety of sources and exhibiting a colourful, and I hope entertaining superstructure which is nevertheless erected on a bed-rock, deep or shallow as may be, of fact. The south coast of Cornwall is covered in another book.

While presenting these stories in my own way, I have preserved their substance unaltered. They derive from books, documents and newspapers which I have read over the years with pleasure and esteem, from conversation, and from information passed on to me by Miss Mary Martyn of Padstow, sister-in-law Mrs. Daphne Nicholls of Wadebridge, Major Tom Ellis O.B.E. of Penpol House, Hayle, cousin Mrs. Mary Main of Lelant, and others. The management of the Headland Hotel, Newquay, were most helpful; while the Royal Institute of Cornwall is always an Aladdin's cave for those who would delve into the duchy's past, with Mr. Douch their infallible guide. My sincere thanks to all. I am especially grateful to Mr. David Clarke, Editor of 'Cornish Life', who has again helped me with advice and with illustrations, and who has allowed me to lift from his magazine parts of an article of mine about Lyonesse. As for my wife Lena, who wrote 'St. Ives Heritage' with me, what could I do without her understanding of Cornish affairs, her encouragement and ever ready aid?

Cousin Mary observed that everybody has at least one good yarn worth the telling. It is indeed a pity to have let so many tales go undiscovered, and to record so few. More next time - and there is always the South Coast book, now ready for the printer. Meanwhile I trust that these stories of our long rugged coastline will interest you, and say something meaningful about the Cornishman and the 'delectable Duchy' that is his home and his inheritance.

Donald Bray

CHAPTER ONE

THE DAMNED, THE LUCKLESS & THE BLESSED

It may be that on Morwenstow cliffs at twilight you will meet an old fellow whom you would take for a fisherman, sea-boots and all, were it not for the white neckerchief tucked into the collar of his guernsey. You will pass, though, rather looking through one another than with that time o' day greeting whereby Cornish folk ordinarily salute the brotherhood of man. For Morwenstow parish, of which he was vicar, was the beloved haunt of Parson-Poet R.S. Hawker for forty of his seventy-one years of eccentric living, and he haunts it still, his death-bed conversion to Rome leaving his immortal self for the time being somewhat 'betwixt and between.' Or so it is said.

However that may be, Parson Hawker lives beyond doubt in the songs and stories he wrote. His "Song of the Western Men" is our Cornish anthem -

"...... And shall Trelawney die?
Here's twenty thousand Cornish men
Will know the reason why!"

As for the strange stories he told of his parish at the northernmost corner of Cornwall, the story of Cruel Coppinger is the strangest. You can come overland into Cornwall without crossing the River Tamar, but only just, travelling south by west out of Devon with dizzy cliffs never far off to your right and the moors piling away to your left. Otherwise old Tamar, that natural frontier which a Cornishman regards as dividing the world into two parts - Cornwall and all the rest - spurns the northern sea beside her birthplace and winds and wantons south-south-east sixty miles or so from Sherston Moor in Morwenstow parish to greet the Channel tides. With the Tamar severing almost the entire county from neighbouring England and the devil fearful, so our forefathers insist, of venturing across lest he be baked in a pasty, small wonder that so many saints have found themselves at home here, all subscribing to Cornish place-names!

But there was that gap, that Achilles knee (look at the map; you could never call it a heel!) to the north. It is no surprise that 'Cruel' Coppinger, a son of the devil if ever there was one, should have joined forces with his father there. Coppinger - and we have it on the authority of R.S. Hawker, Vicar of Morwenstow - swept into Cornwall in a sou'westerly gale in the mid 1700's. The huddle of onlookers on the shore, most of them expectant wreckers, watched in amazement as the master of the labouring craft stripped to the buff, dived into the surf and swam

Morwenstow Church. Courtesy Ray Bishop.

ashore, making light of the turmoil of the waves. With his ship vanishing into the murk the swimmer strode up the beach and snatched from an old woman the red woollen cloak which was the traditional garb of her kind. Thus accoutred he vaulted onto the crupper of a spectator's horse, and seizing the reins urged the beast inland.

The rider thus encircled by the stranger's arms - not unwillingly, for she regarded him with reason enough as a fine figure of a man - was a Miss Dinah Hamlyn. Reaching the Hamlyn home the newcomer introduced himself to her parents as Coppinger, a Dane of wealth and rank. He accepted his host's Sunday suit and a place at the family board as a matter of course, and soon winning the hand of Dinah married her, though not before the untimely death of her father.

Now Coppinger assumed control of the Hamlyn estate and embarked upon that fiendish routine about which talk persisted even in the Rev. Hawker's time, up to ninety years later. The house became the headquarters of 'Cruel' Coppinger's gang of ruffians who turned the parish into hell's playground: while after they had beheaded a Revenue man on the gunnel of a boat and thrown his corpse overboard no officer of the law dared put a foot across the Devon border. Smuggling and piracy were organised on a scale undreamed of even in this region where both had flourished ever since men put to sea. Night after night strange craft would either anchor beyond the surf to ferry their cargoes ashore in small boats, or were guided by signal lanterns into creeks and coves. Moorland tracks converged at Steeple Brink, a three hundred foot headland where an overhang concealed a cave as large, it was said, as Kilkhampton church.

The sole access to Coppinger's Cave was by rope ladder lowered from above. Tales of revelry in this devil's kitchen, even more abandoned than the 'bel tink' (which is Cornish for goings-on) up at the house, were whispered among the cowed villagers. You would find sheep tethered there, fattened on hay and corn for the next debauchery, all stolen from the surrounding farms. There were kegs of brandy and gin stacked against the cave walls, and box upon box of tea, smuggled each one. Sea chests overflowed with plunder. Members of the 'Cruel' gang alone were admitted, all bound by a frightful oath, and parish comment was stifled by savage punishment. Coppinger himself whipped the vicar half to death for saying too much.

The fiend's method of piecemeal extortion from his mother-in-law was typically his own. He would tie his wife to their great four-poster bed, on which so many Hamlyns had lain in peace and love, and offer the old lady the choice of either paying over a portion of her private dower or watching him flog her daughter with a cat o' nine tails. Sooner rather than later she would yield to the blackmail. Coppinger and the hapless Dinah had only one child - a beautiful boy but deaf and dumb, and with a penchant for cruelty which plumbed the depths in the murder of a playmate. But nobody dared to check the wretch, who grew up to be the scourge of the neighbourhood.

The Rev. Hawker names one of the Coppinger ships which supplied the cave at Steeple Brink as the 'Black Prince.' Swift and well armed, she long ravaged the North Cornwall coast, from time to time the pirate chief himself assuming command. On one such occasion he lured a Revenue cutter into pursuing the 'Black Prince' through the shoals around Gull Rock, where it struck and was lost with all hands. But with consummate skill Coppinger piloted his own craft unscathed through the narrowest of channels.

On Christmas Day 1781 it was reported in the 'Gazette' that the 'Black Prince', a Dunkirker (one of the French-Dutch pirate craft hailing from Dunkirk to terrorise British shipping) which for the past two years had been preying on merchantmen along the Cornish seaways, had been brought to battle by the notorious Mounts Bay smuggler Harry Carter in his giant privateer cutter 'Shaftesbury.' In a running fight from St. Ives to Newquay the 'Black Prince' had out-manoeuvred, out-sailed and outfought both Carter and the brand new lugger that was his consort. Carter withdrew from the action holed between wind and water, while the lugger sank with heavy loss. But this is a tale for further down the coast. Now although the reverend chronicler makes no mention of this contemporary journalism, can the 'Black Prince' of the narrative be other than Coppinger's infamous craft?

Landsmen who offended the 'Cruel' gang were shanghaied aboard and compelled either to pay an enormous ransom or 'sign articles' and join the crew. The devil's rather than the King's press-gang! One near-centenarian told Parson Hawker in 1835 that he had to serve two years aboard the pirate ship before his friends could collect the ransom money. Murder, torture and extortion were commonplace in that corner of Cornwall.

But even Coppinger must have his day. As the years passed piracy and smuggling became less rewarding, poor Dinah being lashed at the bedpost more and more often. And the navy was closing in. His passing as described by Hawker is sheer melodrama. A gale, the combers crashing into the cove and the spindrift flying. The wreckers flock down to the foreshore, for how can that full-rigger in the offing but drive ashore? A rocket hisses into the howling wind and bursts over Gull Rock, on the top of which Coppinger appears brandishing his sword. A signal gun answers from the vessel and a boat puts off. The pirate springs onto the thwarts and is brought to his ship, on the way cutting down an oarsman who is too fatigued to pull his weight. Amid thunder and lightning, hail and squalls the ship disappears out to sea, and the son of Satan is gone for ever.

The tales of Coppinger and his gang were told around the firesides and on the bar settles ten thousand times before Parson Hawker recorded them, and doubtless they were embellished in the telling. But in substance the record is all too true, while local wickednesses a century nearer our own days, that the vicar knew about first-hand, were scarcely less alien to today's holiday beaches and the pleasant dwellings which cluster over the moorland where once smugglers trod. Rev. Hawker employed an ancient, retired smuggler as a house servant, Tristram Pentire his name. 'Trim' never understood why good liquor should be taxed rather than something else - though to be sure a thousand and more of the imports of his heyday were already liable for duty. Nor could the old rascal ever accept that the murder of a 'King's man' was other than natural justice.

Excise officer Parminter who went everywhere escorted by a huge dog called Satan was the prime aversion of Trim and his cronies. Man and dog between them had cost the lives of seven smugglers, the hound being trained to carry a gun in its mouth which it brought to its master's aid in a crisis. One ebb tide the freetraders set up an ambush in 'Johnnie Mathoy's hole' on the beach due for a landing. The first boat-load came ashore, whereupon Parminter stormed down as expected, yelling for Satan. But the dog held back for the first time in its life; and as the officer leapt into the boat brandishing his cutlass the men dashed out of the cave and seized him. They held him neck down over the gunnel and - shades of Coppinger! - hacked off his head.

At Tidnacombe Cross away on the moors near the cliff was a rock known by the Saxon name 'Witan Stone', where the elders had once assembled to debate local policy. Here, in a crevice, was the 'gauger's pocket' where, Trim explained to his master, a gauger - an exciseman - could collect the bribe left as the fee for a blind eye. And many a little bag of gold had Trim dropped there in his time. Now was it not unreasonable, he argued, that Parminter and his dog should harass honest men about their work rather than visit the gauger's pocket once in a while? And had the fellow not deserved his fate? Well, it was a point of view.

Certainly the miscreants got little guidance from Rev. Hawker's predecessors. Describing 'the light of other days', he cited one curate who claimed to keep the smugglers from riotous behaviour by holding the lantern for them in the dark of the night. He would be soothed and silenced by a keg of spirits or a chest of tea. And when you consider that his flock would buy in Holland tea at perhaps 7d (3½p) a pound which was sold at the grocer's for five shillings (25p), and that four gallons of best brandy cost about £1 in Roscoff but £4 on passing through customs in England, no doubt the 50p a week cleric felt that the labourer must prove worthy of his hire!

Curate for the lantern and 'four-legged friends' for transport! Smugglers explained to their recording vicar, once they had turned their backs on wickedness - or were past it - how they would shave and grease their ponies to slip easily out of clutching fingers, and load them with a keg or a bundle slung on either flank. A muttered command, a slap, and away the herd would trot, led by a well trained mare to the cache. One equine heroine, who lived to a hoary thirty-seven, had one night led the herd the whole way from Bossinney Haven to Roughtor Point with neither a driver nor a guide. Generally, though, it was Cornish practice to round up the smugglers' four-legged recruits from stables left unlocked, by threat or promise, for the night's work, and to return them by sun-up together with the appropriate share of the exercise, off-loaded in a cavity in the hedge perhaps, or under a slab in the farmyard.

Never until the success of the 'Preventives' put paid to smuggling as the nineteenth century progressed had the Cornish coastal villages lived wholly within the law - and even afterwards who is to say what felonies would be committed whenever chance offered? Wrecking, for instance! Thus when in a January gale in 1865 the Spanish brig 'Juanita', Greenock bound from Venezuela, drove ashore at Duckpool, rescuers found the captain at bay in his cabin with drawn sword, ready to defend his ship against the wreckers. Perhaps with reason. For even without Coppinger and his kind the 'locals', children of wild moor and wilder sea and living at the very verge of subsistence, were always alert for such pickings as came their way and by no means particular as to how they should obtain them.

Early entries in the chronicles of the coast record piracy and plunder in 981, when the Vikings sacked Petrocstowe, today's Padstow. Irish missionaries had founded a monastery there; not a grand abbey but a cluster of stone huts as at their communal hermitage at Glendalough across the Irish Sea. Not long afterwards a saintly Welsh prince named Petroc, whom some regard as the patron saint of Cornwall rather than the tinners' saint Piran, turned up with sixty followers in the Camel estuary after twenty years of absorbing Irish learning, sixth century Ireland then being the centre of western civilisation. Coming ashore at Lodenek Petroc converted the local heathen, with whom the missionaries had presumably had little success, by miraculously striking water out of a rock. The hermit community thereupon made over its settlement - Prideaux Place, or you may know it as Place House, occupies the site today - to St. Petroc and his group. St. Samson, who was in residence at the time, moved on across the Channel with Cornish emigrants to spread the word in Brittany and eventually to found the town of Dol, from whose hereditary stewards descended the Stewart Kings of Scotland and then of England. The Vikings raided Petrocstowe three hundred years later, just before the end of the first Christian millenium, when most of the faithful were expecting the end of the world. The horned marauders swarming from their terrible dragon-headed longships must surely have seemed to have emerged straight from hell. But what of value those pirates could have wrung from the poor monks and the poorer countryside passes belief. The survivors fled to Bodmin and re-established their monastery far enough from the sea for safety.

The Viking raiders may well have sailed from Lundy, Danish for isle of puffins, a dozen miles nor'-nor'-west of Hartland Point and until not so long ago the nigh impregnable haunt of every kind of villain and adventurer. The worst of these were the Mariscoes. These Mariscoes were not, as you might think, a tribe from some barbaric outpost. They were offshoots of the first Plantagenet, father of Henry II no less; for Sir Jordan de Marisco, who held Lundy under Henry, had wed the daughter of the King's natural brother Hamelin. The Marisco family was of the noble French house of Montmorency, the English and Irish branches being known as Monte de Marisco. Four generations of Mariscoes were nuisances to the Crown and ogres to shipping and coastal dwellers within their reach. The last of them was hanged, drawn and quartered for an attempt on the life of Henry III in 1242.

But Lundy pirates still ravaged the Cornish Sea. One of them, a Frenchman, moving in from the sea to plunder Padstow in Crecy year, was repelled by the women of Padstow on 1st May. Sight of the women there, all in the red cloaks such as Coppinger snatched from the old wrecker when he first came ashore, scared them off. This is not to impute any inadequacies of face and form in Padstow's foremothers, but because the pirates mistook the red cloaked dames for soldiers. And goodness knows what they made of the 'Obby 'Oss' of the pagan Spring festival!

Padstow's pirates were not all foreigners. John Piers of Padstow was a rover famous in his day, and with his crew was held in esteem by his fellow countrymen; though had he plagued home waters they might have thought differently. His mother's reputation as a witch was held to account for a lifetime of successful piracy, which spanned the thirty-nine years from 1552 to 1591, when he was killed while about his business. The outstanding exploit of this remarkable rogue was his dominating the Cinque Port of Rye, which in time of war hired out its ships as a substantial proportion of England's fleet, with a couple of Cornish fishing smacks of 35 and 18 tons respectively. A letter from the Mayor of Rye complained in September 1581 that John Piers had been blockading the harbour for a month, "as that none can go forth or come in", while the handful of Padstow desperadoes terrorised the town.

Rye could very well have driven the impudent Cornishmen off, but the privateering fraternity was "unwilling to do the government's work for it." You can guess why: in 1577 Queen Elizabeth had commissioned privateers to hunt pirates in home waters, and the privateersmen of Rye had not been awarded a full enough share in this lucrative pursuit. Why then do the job unpaid? It would have been the solid citizens and not the roving interests of the ancient port from whom the Padstow pirates topped up their treasure chests, then withdrawing before their luck ran out.

Piers was captured 'by chance' (a pirate like a politician has secret enemies everywhere!) at an anchorage where he was normally safe, Studland Bay just south of Poole harbour. He was committed to

Padstow Harbour c. 1900. Courtesy Mrs. D. Nicholls.

Dorchester gaol to await trial and the short voyage to Execution Dock at the tidemark, preceded by the silver oar which customarily headed a pirate's procession to the gallows. But a bribe to the warder, and Piers was away to sea, back on the beat again. A colourful character, this Piers of Padstow, and not by the standards of his calling a murderous one!

For all that the cliffs hereabouts are grim, and that the sea rages dreadfully when a gale comes hurtling in from the west or the north, there are golden sands and blue skies a-plenty, and seas as gentle as a sleeping child. Nor are all the tales told of these parts and the folk who live here black and violent. Piracy along this stretch of coast was checked for a century and a half when Charles I's navy drove the rovers from their lair at Lundy. Though with the Scillies welcoming them at the far end of the county and pickings ever more promising beckoning across the Atlantic, the respite favoured only the border Cornish, and that but briefly; for fresh alarums were soon to sound from a different quarter.

When King Charles's fleet, shortly to turn its coat and serve Cromwell, cleared Lundy Sir Bevil Grenville was Lord of Stowe, the North Cornwall home of Elizabethan Sir Richard of the 'Revenge.' Sir Bevil was the Galahad of the Cavaliers; for much good came out of North Cornwall - good, true and magnificent, like that huge fellow you can see portrayed in Truro Museum, resplendent in his red uniform and grasping a halberd as if it were a walking staff: Anthony Payne, the Cornish giant, all seven foot four inches of him, and every inch of it honourable. Stratton, the border town a mile or so above Bude, was his birthplace and Stowe his home until as Sir Bevil's most trusted retainer he went to war for his King.

Anthony Payne was not, as you might suppose from the bulk of him, clumsy and uncouth. He was nimble, well favoured and astute, literate above the common, and of a kind and generous disposition. And his strength was proverbial. One Christmas Eve my lady sat chafing in the great hall at Stowe because the donkey boy despatched to the woods for logs had not returned. Off strode the giant, soon to reappear with donkey, load and all, over his shoulders and dump the lot at the hearthside before the amazed company with a merry "Ass and fardel, ass and fardel for my lady's yule!"

The giant was at his master's side when Sir Bevil won the battle of Stratton Hill, and again at Lansdown near Bath, scene of another royalist triumph. But at the outset Sir Bevil was killed. Payne mounted John, the sixteen year old Grenville heir, on Sir Bevil's charger and at his bridle led the Stowe troop to victory. When all was done, he described the scene in a touching letter to his bereaved mistress.

Young John Grenville was created Earl of Bath at the Restoration and appointed Governor of the Plymouth garrison. There Anthony Payne, much admired by the new king, was promoted Halberdier of the Guns, a sort of Regimental Sergeant Major, in which capacity Charles II had the big man's portrait painted by the famous court artist Sir Godfrey Kneller. This is the painting you will see at Truro; and a rugged contrast it is to the pretty ladies Kneller was commonly commissioned to immortalise. Long afterwards, when a Stuart queen shared England's throne with a Dutch king and it was the fashion to belittle the sovereigns Payne had so staunchly served, the ageing though still supple giant fought a duel on Plymouth ramparts with a noted swordsman, for an insult to the martyred Charles, and ran him through.

Anthony Payne spent his retirement at home at Stratton. He died in 1691 in the house in which he was born - and they could not get his massive body through the door of his room and down the stairs. So the flooring was sawn away and he was lowered with rope and pulley to the room below. Relays of bearers bore him to his tomb outside the south wall of Stratton church while the bells of the tower tolled. In Parson Hawker's youth the vault collapsed, but within it was no sign of the Cornish giant. Gone like the giants of legend before him, but with his strength never misused nor any taint of meanness to dishonour that great frame!

Cornwall could claim its intellectual giants too - a gratifying concourse considering that its population was far less, even, than today's when many an industrial town counts more citizens within its bounds than are contained in all our 1400 square miles. In none of these gifted sons of Cornwall did the genius of invention glow more brightly than in Goldsworthy Gurney; and if his fame is dim it is because luck and big business were dead set against him.

Gurney was born at Treator near Padstow on St. Valentine's Day 1793 and was educated at Truro Grammar School. This school had at the time an exceptionally able headmaster; for however the Rev. Cornelius Cardew, vicar of St. Erme nearby, may have shrugged off his clerical responsibilities - as absentee vicar of Lelant, too, he paid a curate £45 a year to run, more or less, the extensive group of parishes of Lelant, St. Ives and Towednack - he raised a crop of brilliant pupils ranging from the scientist Sir Humphry Davy to Admiral Edward Pellow, Viscount Exmouth; household names both of them.

In the school holidays Gurney would often stay with his relative the vicar of St. Erth. A neighbour of the vicar was Mr. Davies Giddy of Tredrea, another Cornishman of exceptional talents who was destined, with a change of surname to Gilbert, to succeed Davy as President of the Royal Society. With a keen eye to incipient genius Mr. Giddy encouraged the youngster to visit him. Another constant visitor to Tredrea was the engineer of a nearby copper mine, Richard Trevithick no less, inventor of the world's first practical steam locomotive, who came to consult his mentor on the mathematical problems involved in harnessing pressurised steam, and whose experiments intrigued the schoolboy. On leaving school to study medicine he kept in touch with Trevithick.

Gurney married in 1814 and worked up a promising practice in the Wadebridge area, but after six years of it he decided that the placebo and the scalpel were not for him, and that with greater profit to both himself and mankind he should employ his talents as a scientist. So he moved to London, and after three years of lecturing began his own experiments with steam.

Gurney was concerned that the pioneers of steam got so little power out of the vast potential at their command. Thus the famous and fortunate George Stephenson, giving evidence to a parliamentary committee, stated that his locomotive travelled at no more than six miles an hour, while his colleague Nicholas Wood added in his railway book of 1829 that it was ridiculous to expect anything faster. And so it would have been had not the Padstow inventor realised and resolved the problem. For already in 1829 Gurney had patented a steam coach which incorporated his own improvements, and Wood had scarcely uttered his pessimistic edict when there was the Gurney steam carriage charging along at a reckless 15 miles per hour. The Cornishman had not wasted the nine years since forsaking medicine, and Wood was let into the secret of this incredible speed. Stephenson incorporated the device, without acknowledgement to its inventor, in his historic 'Rocket', which thereupon streaked along the track at nearly 30 m.p.h. He took the whole credit for it, and the emoluments thereof.

Gurney's workshop had been open to the public throughout, and so to exploitation. Like many another genius he kept his brains under his hat but not in his pocket. What he had spotted in Trevithick's engine was that, even with the tallest chimney, a down draught prevented the furnace from staying at full blast. It was a difficulty even more pronounced in a locomotive. Your boiler pressure dropped and however bravely you started off you could not build up a speed. Gurney's solution was to fit jets which spurted steam up the funnel or chimney, reversed the down-draught, and created a vacuum which sucked a steady flow of air into the furnace and so maintained a head of steam. This steam-jet system was first installed in blast furnaces and factories, and as early as 1824 in a couple of steamboats too. In France it was similarly applied, again without benefit to the inventor.

So Gurney had turned his mind to steam carriages. His prodigiously fast trip from Bath to London and back in 1829 - he drove himself - was the longest machine-powered road journey yet. It ought to be ranked with Bleriot's flying the Channel. Two more years and the Gloucester steam-bus service was plying five times daily between Gloucester and Cheltenham. The old stage coach had had its day. But had it? The stage coach lobby asserted itself in Parliament, clapping on the steam carriage a turnpike toll more than five times what the stage coach paid. So four months and four thousand miles after its inception, and with the safe and speedy transport of three thousand satisfied passengers, this promising venture collapsed. Then a Parliamentary Select Committee decided that steam carriages served the national interest and recommended that the crippling levy be lifted. You may be sure that coach owners, turnpike trustees and the whole company of coachmen and ostlers and innkeepers at the staging posts were not going to stand for that; that even the horses said "Neigh" too! Parliament turned the recommendation down and would not allow Gurney even his expenses. Thus the luckless Goldsworthy Gurney having abandoned a promising practice, and backed his brain-child with his entire £30,000 personal fortune, after five years of experiment and toil was ruined.

Gurney is particularly remembered in Bude for the lamp he patented in 1838 for the lighthouse in the haven, introducing an oxygen jet into an encircling oil, and later coal-gas, flame and thus achieving such a glow as had never before pierced the murk of the gale. Gurney's lamp came to be fitted in lighthouses from the Pentlands to Finisterre; but you'll find scant mention anywhere of the Bude light nor of Goldsworthy Gurney. His original oil flame had proved too costly to impress the Brethren of Trinity House. The old fish-tail burner some of us still recall was a domestic development of the lamp in the lighthouse, air being infused into burning gas to produce a white flame. It was to illumine many a parlour and passageway until someone popped a gas mantle on the jet; and this in itself was a variant of another Gurney discovery - that if you direct an oxy-hydrogen blowpipe onto a cylinder of lime you get a dazzling light; limelight.

Ships at sea are further indebted to the Padstow genius who asked Why? and then How? on so many occasions, for the flash of the lighthouse as dusk steals over the coast. For each lighthouse emitting a different number or duration of flashes is his brain child too. The lighthouse identifies itself thereby on the darkest night, when there is no sign of land, so that the navigator knows the rock or headland on which he has taken a bearing, and as the next lighthouse comes into view plots his exact position. Moreover by studying lightning conductors Gurney foresaw the electric telegraph long before its time.

Take a good look at Bude Castle. Gurney built it in 1850 on a concrete platform, to demonstrate the feasibility of building on sand, and lived in it for a while. Now skyscrapers in earthquake zones of the world survive by the same method. Bude Castle still sits snug on its foundations, as the municipal offices of the joint Bude-Stratton Council. He found other uses for his steam jet, extinguishing fires in coal mines and in ventilating mines and the network of sewers which was multiplying beneath every town in the kingdom. He also invented steam central heating, and this he installed with gas lighting in the old House of Commons, while in 1854 he was appointed superintendent of lighting, heating and ventilation in the

Bude Harbour. c. 1850. Courtesy Royal Institute of Cornwall.

Sir Goldsworthy Gurney's Bude Castle. Courtesy Royal Institute of Cornwall.

Palace of Westminster.

And this was all Gurney gained from his phenomenal fertility of ideas and the intellectual capacity to translate them into practice: a job at Westminster and nine years later a knighthood which a paralytic stroke almost immediately prevented the luckless genius from ever enjoying. He languished helpless in his house at Reeds, in Poughill by Bude, for twelve years, tended by his daughter Anna - yet another of that unsung spinsterhood who dedicate their lives to ailing parents. Sir Goldsworthy Gurney died on the last day of February 1875 at the age of 82, with his steam jet, and his gaslight and heating systems benefiting millions and endowing millionaires, and with his lamp shining out to sea from the lighthouse so near his deathbed. He was buried at Launcells, a lonely church close by. And if ever you doubt that good fortune is a better friend to a man than mere genius, there lies your mere genius to prove it.'

SIR GOLDSWORTHY GURNEY OF PADSTOW

Hi Coachie, hold your six-in-hand!
  Stage passengers, sit tight!
Goldsworthy Gurney's motor car
  Comes puffing into sight.

Coke's cracking in the furnace, Gurney's
  Steam jet's in the flue,
And my, how wheels and pistons fly -
  And smoke and ashes too!

It's eighteen-twenty-nine, July;
  Steam Carriage Number one,
Tiller and clutch at the master's touch,
  Makes the Bath-London run.

The turnpike keepers grab the toll,
  Turn the pike, spit and shout
"No nags? No reins? Just stink and flames!
  Hell's chariot is out!"

Fifteen milestones every hour;
  Horses shy, dogs bark.
Water and fuel at London Tower
  Then back to Bath by dark.

The Cotswold steam-bus next, which plies
Five trips a day, of course is
Now the fast, fashionable mode -
A fig for coach and horses!

But parliamentary coach and turn-
Pike lobbies merge to stop it;
No steam contraptions for our roads!
Poor Gurney, broke, must drop it.

He got a job at Westminster
(Who drove too soon too quick)
Steam-heating Parliament; was dubbed
A knight when old and sick.

They buried him at Launcells,
This Padstow engineer
Who wedded speed to power and brought
The horseless carriage here.

Trengrouse, Trevithick, Opie,
Davy, Adams - a sixth star
Illumes your Age of Genius. He
Conceived the motor car.

Davy lamps tarnish on the shelf,
Diesels devour the track,
But petrol-starved, what odds we'll see
Gurney's steam carriage back?

But there is the other side of the coin on display, too, in this rugged, romantic, bitter-sweet corner of Cornwall. Thomasine Bonaventure; even her name implies good fortune, and likely enough that is how she came by it, for Bonaventure is hardly a name usual among the cottagers of North Cornwall, even with such as in the middle ages bore surnames. Thomasine Bonaventure, the shepherdess with the luck of Cinderella and the virtues, at least in later life, of a saint! She was born in 1450, of humble parents, at Week St. Mary inland of Crackington Haven and the highest cliffs in Cornwall, and blossomed into a girl of exceptional beauty. So much so that one day, when she was tending her flock beside what passed for a highway in those days, Richard Bunsby, a merchant passing by about his business, fell in love with her there and then and implored her to return to London with him. He must settle affairs with mother and father first, she said. This he did. assuring them that their daughter would be employed in his house as a servant with good wages and her future taken care of.

So up to town went the country lass, with the great wide world opening up before her and undreamt of jollifications on the way. In the merry household that was typical of mercers at the height of the wool trade, and with her sweet nature and willing ways, she easily accommodated herself to the duties required of her. What Mrs. Bunsby thought of the new and lovely wench we can only guess; but shortly afterwards the dame died, and Mr. Bunsby took Thomasine Bonaventure to wife.

Three years on, and Richard Bunsby rejoined his first wife, leaving his entire wealth to his comely widow. Suitors flocked around her like the sheep on her hills by the Cornish sea, and Thomasine's choice fell on a merchant adventurer eminent in the City, Master John Gall. He raised no objection to his wife's donating from her fortune, of which he was now custodian, considerable sums for poor relief in distant Week St. Mary, and the saint within that equisite frame begins to shine through.

Five more years, and it was the turn of Master Gall to exchange her charms for the more durable values of eternity. Thomasine's third husband was John Percival Esquire, Sheriff of London in 1488 and knighted by King Henry VII on becoming Lord Mayor next year. But his days too were numbered, whereupon Thomasine, childless for all her three marriage beds of increasing magnificence, devoted her enormous wealth to good works home in North Cornwall - road and bridge building, feeding and clothing the poor, endowing maidens, relieving prisoners and in general earning the praise and prayers of the neighbourhood, whatever folk may have said, as being villagers they surely did, about the manner of her leaving home.

At Week St. Mary she founded a chantry and a free school with a library and admirable accommodation for teachers and pupils, and a yearly endowment to meet all needs. It is supposed that she built a church there too, or at least its tower, all long in ruin. But everything went with the Reformation, though Stratton churchwardens' accounts for 1513 survive to show that on "My Lady Parcyvale's meneday", when prayers were to be said for the repose of her soul, two shillings and two pence were to be paid for two priests - and for bread and ale.

CHAPTER TWO

CONFLICT, THE LEGION AND A BRIDGE OR TWO

On Christmas Day, 1781, a British privateer with what remained of her bowsprit pointing to the sky slid beneath a tumbling sea after being "beaten to pieces" in a fight off Newquay. The victor, the cutter 'Black Prince', was reported in the newspapers as a Dunkirk privateer which had played havoc with the shipping of the coast ever since France, Spain and Holland joined the American colonies in their war against the mother country. With better reason, though, we may consider her none other than Cruel Coppinger's pirate craft.

Shortly before this engagement the 'Black Prince' had even anchored within St. Ives harbour, to the terror of the inhabitants to whom she was indeed nothing but a pirate. For in '79 the master of one of the aggressor's victims recognised his captors as being neither French, Spanish, Dutch nor Yankee Doodle, but as men well-known locally, while the ship, for all that she had hoisted the stars and stripes when giving chase, was a familiar smuggling cutter. Had she been the privateer she claimed to be, she would have sold her prizes across the Channel and handed over her prisoners for internment, this being the universal requirement for vessels cruising under letters of marque. However the 'Exeter Flying Post' listed five captures by this competent rover, all of which were ransomed, crews and all. And now this scourge of the North Cornish coast lay off St. Ives; whereupon Mr. John Knill, Collector of Customs there, sent a rider post-haste to Captain Harry Carter then lying off Newlyn. He was to sail 'round the land' with his own great cutter 'Shaftesbury', the equal in speed, armament and manpower of the foe, and his new and more heavily gunned lugger 'Phoenix', to destroy the 'Black Prince.'

Captain Carter, commodore as it were of the famous Carter Brothers' smuggling fleet, was loth to go. True, the larger Carter vessels were licensed privateers, though how they had got their papers only heaven and secret but mightily influential backers 'up to Lunnon' knew! Yet deliberately to bring a rival to battle with no prospect of reward beyond at best a battered hull and repairs guaranteed to put fat, submissive prizes and a 'run' cargo or two out of question for months, and with glory as the sole return for death and injury, was well enough for the King's navy but not for private warships in the game for profit. However no naval ship patrolled between St. Ives and the Lizard, while to ignore such a magnate as John Knill, no enemy to smugglers beneath his official exterior, was unwise. So Captain Harry yo'ho'd his anchors out of the drowned forest seabed in Mounts Bay and went to war. "It was not a very agreeable business," he wrote, "notwithstanding for fear to offend the collector, we put round the both vessels to St. Ives Roade."

There Christmas Eve found the larger part of the two ships' companies celebrating ashore, an indulgence hardly to the credit of a commander with his opponent in the offing. Doubtless his control of his men wore thin once easy pickings were out of reckoning. Captain Harry Carter was a good seaman and an efficient 'free trader,' but not a popular leader, an inadequacy his penal restrictions on swearing aboard ship did nothing to redress. For Harry - and this may fortify your opinion as to a Cornishman's, or at least an eighteenth century Cornishman's, assessment of virtue - was a local preacher whose pulpit tirades called to repentance many a sinner who relished nothing more than a hellfire sermon, and a noggin of the Captain's moonshine rum afterwards. And of course it would happen that with so many British privateers-men greeting the happy morn at St. Ives, or come to that, home at Mounts Bay two or three hours' walking distance away, the 'Black Prince' hove in sight.

To Carter's and the local fishermen's credit scratch crews were enlisted and the squadron gave chase. 'Shaftesbury', the flagship, mounted 16 cannon though lamentably short of the gunners of her 80 complement to man them. 'Phoenix' under Captain Dewen had 20 guns but only 31 of her ship's company. The pirate carried 16 guns and 60 seamen, disciplined and trained as you would expect of a Coppinger crew and blooded in battle, and as the pursuers came within range she opened fire. A typical North Cornwall winter gale was working up, yet despite the lop on the sea her shooting was deadly. Not so that of the privateers, whose gun crews were mostly untried and undrilled. Harry Carter, under fire for the first time, concealed his fear and "stood on the companion until the wad of the enemies' shot flew in fire aboute me" (they must have been pretty close alongside) "and I suppose the wind of the shot struck me down on the deck as the shot took in the mainsail right in line with me. One of my officers helpt me up, ... and he would not suffer me to go there nomore. This was a great salvation, and that of God, and not the only one; for all so many hundreds of shot have flyed around me, I never received somuch as a blemish in one of my fingers."

Captain Harry's lack of experience in ship-to-ship action, let alone in squadron tactics, nullified his superior fire power. After a running fight up the Cornish coast for three hours the 'Shaftesbury's' rigging had been shot up and her hull was damaged. Moreover Captain Dewen had broken off the engagement. Carter deemed it prudent to investigate, and the 'Black Prince' showed her heels to her discomfited opponents. Christmas night must have been merry indeed for the rover as she sped through the gale back to her lair. Meanwhile Captain Harry caught up with his consort at five that evening and found the lugger in a bad way. She had been holed between wind and water, and all hands were busy pumping and bailing as Dewen sought to make Padstow through the rising sea. Not a hope! An hour later he gave orders to launch the boat and abandon ship. This evolution was not conducted without panic, as a result of which the lifeboat filled with water, and the 'Phoenix' sank stern first down to Davy Jones's locker, leaving thirty-two men floundering among the wave-crests. Carter got his own boat over the side in seamanlike fashion, and seventeen of the 'Phoenixes' were picked up as the cloudy twilight faded. The remaining fifteen were never seen again though the cutter, hove-to, searched through the dark for more survivors until Carter was "obliged to get the cuttar under a double reefed trysail, a heavy gale of wind ensuing, and bore up for the Mumbles."

At Padstow in 1900 the enemy, as so often, was the sea. Padstow, "the best haven in the north parte of the Shyre," the Elizabethan map-maker Norden noted, is "barred with the sea sand on the estate." A few years afterwards Richard Carew commended the sand bars, building up on their rocky base, as being "sufficiently strong to resist the ocean's threatening billows;" for within their shelter, Norden had continued, rode "manie Ships and of greate burden." They ride there today, though no longer of a 'burden' to arouse comment. But at the harbour entrance how those 'threatening billows' can rage, crashing and curdling upon hidden sands which grip a ship in the clutch of death while the sea pounds her to bits.

Even when the Camel estuary lay smooth and silvery as the beaten pewter some Cornish sideboards display, still through the ages ships found their graveyard there. For beneath that alluring surface where pleasure craft bustle in 'the season' the sand bars lurk, largest of all the Doombar (dune-bar), almost a mile of it, not to be traversed by deep-sea keel "without a skilfull Pylate." According to legend the bar came there through the curse of an angry mermaid. You never get far from mermaids in Old Cornwall! Whatever its cause, that bar has destroyed more fine craft than any sand bar other than the Goodwins in the whole kingdom. If every listed wreck in the Camel estuary were to rise from those sands of doom in a maritime doomsday, you would not see the sea for spectral spars.

Cornwall's first lifeboat was stationed at Padstow in 1827, since when it is the ancient port's boast that no call for help from a vessel in sight of its cliffs has ever been denied. There have been times when the lifeboatmen themselves met the fate they strove so selflessly to fend off from others. You will see in the parish church a memorial to five gallant lifeboatmen who perished in 1867, when attempting to rescue the crew of the 'Georgiana' aground on the Doombar. "The Lord hath His way," the inscription reads, "in the whirlwind and in the storm."

They will tell you on the quay about the later Padstow lifeboat disasters. It was soon after dark on 11th April 1900 when the rockets, booming above the blast of the wind and illuming the scurrying cloud-wrack with a brief shower of stars, summoned the lifeboats crews - there

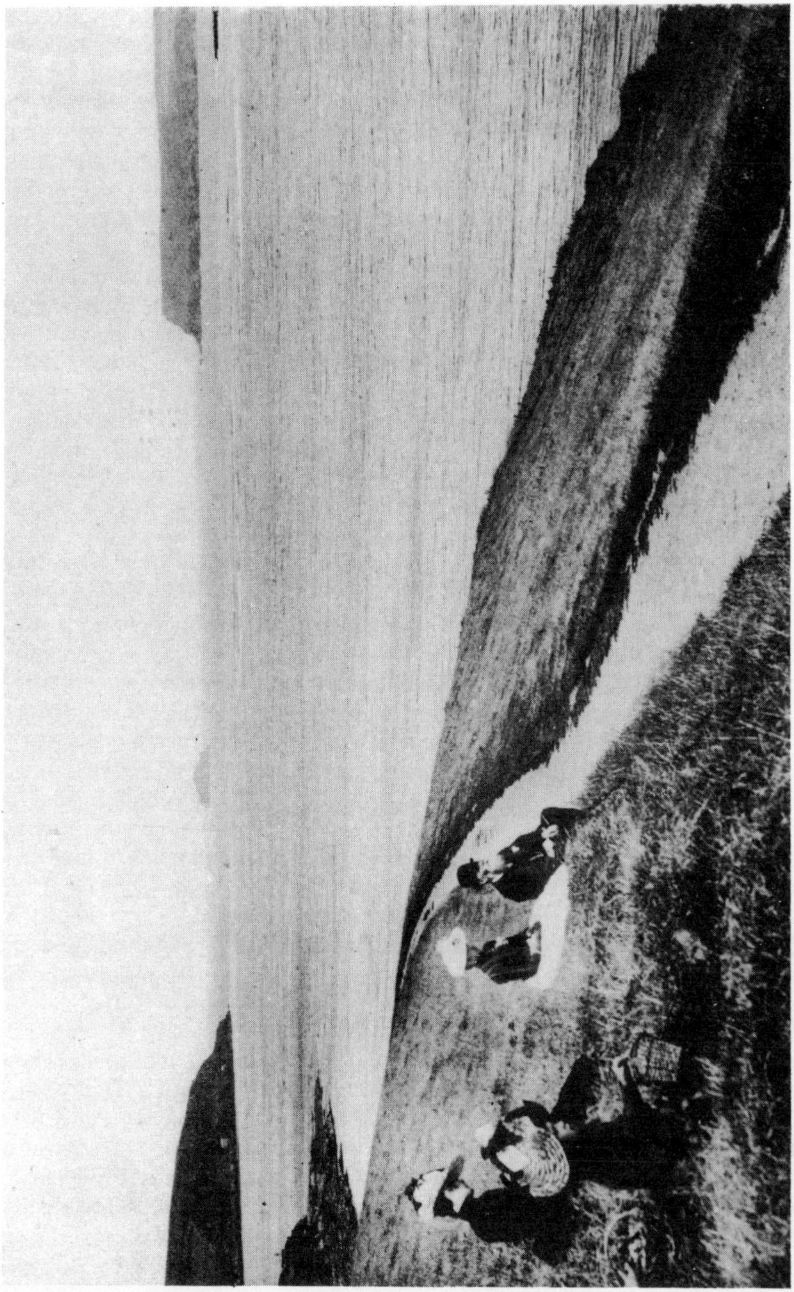

Padstow Picnic c. 1900. Looking along the Doombar. *Courtesy Mrs. D. Nicholls.*

were two boats on the station - and sent the rocket and breeches-buoy team hurrying to Trebetherick with their apparatus. For the East Coast trawler 'Peace and Plenty' was in trouble off the bar, and seas thundering upon the reef more furiously than any Padstow man could remember were not to deter the town's utmost attempts at rescue. So with the help of men and women summoned too by the maroons from quiet lamplight into a night that was to be wilder, and seem longer, than any night known before, the rowing lifeboat 'Arab' and the new steam lifeboat 'James Stevens' were launched into the estuary.

Coxswain Brown took the 'Arab' through a channel straight across the Doombar, navigable only by a boat of shallow draught. By this time the trawler was aground and giant combers were hammering her. The lifeboat forced her way slowly in the teeth of the wind through the turmoil on the bar, the spray sheeting onto the backs of the rowers as they laboured desperately to reach the Lowestoft fishermen before their ship yielded to the sea. A vain effort! A breaker avalanched into the open boat, sluicing eight of her crew overboard, oars and all. Somehow they struggled back aboard, but with only three oars left and not a hope of aiding the 'Peace and Plenty,' their own survival was chancey indeed. Eventually Cox'n Brown, now with but a single serviceable oar, contrived to steer his waterlogged boat into a little creek. As she came in the rocks smashed the rudder and jagged the side of the lifeboat, and there she was found next morning. But it was not the 'Arab's' crew that the sea was to claim that night. Every man stumbled through the surf and over the rocks to land.

Meanwhile the 'James Stevens,' pride of the R.N.L.I. and too large for the passage across the bar, rounded the reef to close from seaward - a perilous manoeuvre, for she no longer met the sea head on but presented her beam and then her stern to the onslaught. Cox'n Grubb with a skill born of a lifetime afloat completed the turn and steamed for the trawler and the swamped 'Arab.' So deep were the troughs that every time she dipped between the towering crests her masthead light vanished from shore view. Then a monstrous breaker came rearing out of the night on the lifeboat's quarter. It pooped her, rolled her over, flung every man on deck into the maelstrom, trapped the engine room crew in the dark horror of scalding steam and a scattering furnace. Daybreak disclosed the 'James Stevens' wrecked too, a shapeless hulk washed up into a cave. Three alone survived of her crew of eleven. Cox'n Grubb was not one of them. They heard him calling his son among the waves which drowned them both.

While the "whirlwind and the storm" were destroying Padstow's two lifeboats on the bar, the rocket team had set up their Trengrouse apparatus at Trebetherick and fired a line across to the 'Peace and Plenty,' or what remained of her. Five trawlermen were hauled through the surf and up the cliff. The others of her crew of eight were lost. So besides three vessels built particularly to withstand the fury of inshore waters, the sea

Padstow Lifeboat Edmund Harvey 1901 to 1928, replaced the wrecked lifeboat Arab.
Courtesy Royal Institute of Cornwall.

claimed eleven brave men that night of gigantic waves pounding the North Cornish coast. A stone cross, curiously and beautifully carved in the Celtic style, is their memorial.

A memorial of a quite different sort, evoking the pride but not the sorrow, came to light in one of those elegant modern bungalows on Trebetherick cliffs which overlook the Doombar. It lay hidden in a photograph album, and animated forgotten shadows like the murmur of the sea in a shell.

Did you know that in October 1938 a thousand members of the British Legion, whose banners you watch paraded at the Albert Hall every November, were mobilised and armed with walking sticks to confront the Nazis in central Europe? Unbelievable, but true! It happened to be at Trebetherick, and it could have been anywhere else in Cornwall or indeed in the whole national network of the Legion, that family photographs disclosed what must have been the most suppressed British non-event of all the pre-war manoeuvrings. These photographs show the British Legion Volunteer Plebiscite Police Force kitting out, taking the oath at Olympia, marching through London on 8th October, ash sticks in hand, and embarking on what was acknowledged to be a most hazardous enterprise. Ex-Sergeant O.P.S. Martyn, in whose family album these photographs have puzzled his daughter ever since they came into her possession, for her father never enlightened her, himself appears among the Cornish contingent. He was one of four legionaries selected to represent his branch.

This extraordinary mobilisation, which took place soon after the Admiralty had called up and then disbanded the Fleet Reserve, was a consequence of that web of deception through which Hitler's war exploded upon a stunned world. In 1938 it was the German Fuehrer's designs on Czechoslovakia that set the embassies in a whirl from Moscow to Montevideo. Czechoslovakia was a stronghold of democracy, an ally of Great Britain and France, not to be subverted as Austria had been. She was moreover a principal arsenal of the free nations, and as such necessary to the Nazis if only to prevent her armaments from being used against the Reich.

A strip of Czechoslovakia along the German border, the Sudetenland, contained as you would expect a fair sprinkling of Germans, and these were to prove the Achilles heel of the doomed Czechs. Berlin stirred up the Sudetenland to demand self-determination, by means of a plebiscite which would be so manipulated that the German minority would take over, and provide Hitler with an undefended frontier across which to invade and subjugate. In the face of vacillating opposition from Great Britain and France, Hitler decided to chance his arm. He had done it before on three occasions and got away with it. So he issued an ultimation to Prague; surrender the Sudetenland, or else......!

The Czechs were confident of the support of their allies. But when

British Legion embarks in SS Dunera en route to Czechoslovakia
Courtesy Miss Mary Martyn.

The Legion on the March - Courtesy Miss Mary Martyn.

an alarmed Neville Chamberlain, the British Prime Minister, flew to Hitler in his mountain eyrie he agreed, subject to the plebiscite being independently supervised, to deliver up his ally's disputed territory as the price of peace. You may remember the tumultuous applause which greeted the Prime Minister when he emerged from his plane at London Airport, brandishing Hitler's signature and proclaiming "Peace in our time."

This plebiscite concession that Chamberlain gained, or thought he had gained, was that an international commission should determine Germany's new and final frontiers. Lord Halifax at the Foreign Office hit upon the Legion, with its seasoned membership of ex-servicemen, as a happy contribution to the commission. That is how ex-Sergeant O.P.S. Martyn, respected timber merchant of Wadebridge, up-river from Padstow, found himself on the Paddington train with twenty other Cornishmen, bound to Olympia for enrolment as a volunteer policeman for service overseas.

The Cornish battalion, for so each county group was designated, comprised in common with all the others ex-servicemen of every rank and every occupation - or none. They mucked in together, sharing food, fatigues and parades alike and foreshadowing those Civil Defence Volunteers who were later to become the Home Guard, 'Dad's Army.' It fell to O.P.S. Martyn, as a senior officer of the Legion, to drill the Cornish squad. Among them stood the Right Reverend the Lord Bishop of Truro, Dr. Hunkin, elected - and his chauffeur with him - by the Truro Branch.

The thousand volunteers appointed by their fellow Old Comrades to re-enter the Europe they had endured in misery and left in triumph, twenty years before, were issued with police uniforms, peaked caps and badges, and yellow armbands such as mark today those auxiliaries of the constabulary, the traffic wardens. Each volunteer gripped the stout ash stick that he had had to provide for himself. Married men received government pay of £3-15s. (£3.75) a week, and single men £3 - which indicates a wife's upkeep in those Spartan days - together with rations and accommodation - Spartan too, you may be sure. They spent six days and nights at Olympia, earnestly preparing for the great adventure, and then boarded the British India liner 'Dunera' which was to ferry them across the Channel. One of Sergeant Martyn's photographs shows the Legion filing up the gangplank with kitbag, water bottle, and overcoat and waterproof sheet slung like a bandolier across their shoulders, the B.E.F. all over again, except for the blue of the uniform, the walking stick that replaced the rifle, and no puttees.

A day passed. A second. A third. Still the 'Dunera' hugged the dock. Then "the British Legion Volunteer Police, selected for special police duty in plebiscite areas of Czechoslovakia" with such high hopes, had to file ashore, and were piled into the trains, the adventure ended before it had begun. Whereupon a bewildered Sergeant Martyn found himself back in the bosom of his family less than a fortnight after leaving home.

What had happened? The Nazis occupied the Sudetenland without the supervised plebiscite, which had been promised only to keep Chamberlain quiet. Then they proceeded by assassination and intimidation to scoop the rest of the dismembered and bitterly disillusioned State into their net. The democracies duped again! However Lord Halifax sent each member of the British Legion Force a fine, firm letter emphasising that peace as well as war demanded hard work and unremitting effort. It does not appear that O.P.S. Martyn kept his.

The mobilisation of the Legion came to nothing. But it deserves honourable mention after all these years. In view of what every legionary expected of Hitler's bully boys it took guts to volunteer, to thrust one's head into the lion's jaws. There was no 1938 medal for ex-Sergeant Martyn of Wadebridge; but his photographs testify to his courage and resolution - his and that of the twenty one Cornish Old Comrades and of the thousand old soldiers the British Legion marshalled at their country's need from all over the United Kingdom.

The ex-Sergeant's grandfather had been typical of a new breed of business men who stood up to the squirearchy as the industrial revolution reached its peak. In 1847 Thomas Martyn crossed swords -figuratively! - with the redoubtable Sir William Molesworth, 8th Baronet, notable scholar, twice Member of Parliament for East Cornwall, and master of Pencarrow. Pencarrow is the handsome eighteenth century Palladian mansion you may have visited when open to the public; it is now the home of Sir John Molesworth St. Aubyn. The estate Elizabeth I had granted to the Molesworths included the Wadebridge, or Ward bridge, that gave its name to the town. It was this bridge that was the bone of contention between timber merchant and squire, Mr. Martyn seeing it as serving the needs of the developing town, whereas to Sir William it was primarily his personal access to interests across the river.

The Wadebridge was begun about 1485, when the middle ages were merging into modern times and Columbus was within seven years of discovering America. It had in its day displayed not only the heads of executed criminals but the body of the martyred Cuthbert Mayne, swung from the central of its seventeen arches. By the mid-nineteenth century the uses of the bridge, mercifully restrained in one respect, fell far short of requirements in another. Only a couple of pack animals could squeeze past each other, while a single carriage or cart occupied the bridge for the whole of its 320 foot transit.

The transport of timber along it was a slow and vexatious process, the quay at which it was imported as 'baulks' - trimmed tree trunks - from Norway being on the Pencarrow side of the Camel, while the Martyn yard was on the west bank. Consequent blocks and hold-ups were an annoyance

CORNISH CONTINGENT - BRITISH LEGION VOLUNTEER POLICE FORCE - SUDETEN PLEBISCITE 1938

Courtesy Miss Mary Martyn.

Left to Right. Standing: F.L. Mitchell, M.S. Pascoe. E. Weary. T.G. Rouncefield. W.B. Watts. L.G. Snell. V.G. Prideaux. C. Marshall. O.P.S. Martyn. J.F. Hallett. J.T. James.

Centre: A.L. Young. G.A. Kitto. The Bishop of Truro. W.J. Dunstan. D.J. Ede. Capt. P.A. Wellman. A.T. Weekes. T.W. Chubb.

Front Row: Capt. R.J.V. Falkner. M. Peters.

Wadebridge c. 1900. *Courtesy Mrs. D. Nicholls.*

The Bridge at Chapel Amble *Copyright Ivan Rabey.*

to both the timber company and everybody else except, perhaps, Sir William who could take his time. Mr. Martyn accordingly waited upon the Squire, requesting him to widen the Wadebridge and offering to pay half the cost himself. Sir William refused. An accident thereupon occurred. Midway across the ancient bridge a 'drag', massively loaded and drawn by six horses, shed a wheel. The traffic block was so effective that it took a whole week to dislodge the drag and the jammed baulks. Meanwhile the angry Squire missed an important meeting in Truro and was cut off from magisterial and estate commitments on the far side.

But he widened the bridge.

Below Wadebridge a creek of the Camel estuary reaches inland to Amble village. Time was when a barge could be rowed all the way to Amble at high tide, passing under Trewornan bridge where the Wadebridge to Port Isaac road crosses the creek. Smuggling being a major industry of Old Cornwall, it will not surprise you that few barges travelled to Amble, which was so relatively free of Revenue patrolmen, without hiding a keg or two of spirits and a box of tea among the cargo. At Lands, the ancestral home of the Webbers, the bottom of a green glass bottle had been inserted in the outer wall of the cider press, a sure sign to those in the know, as in Devon, that the house was in those days a distribution centre for contraband.

As was then common along the whole Cornish coast, from Bude westward and 'round the land' up to Cawsand and Kingsand, the highways, such as they were, were plagued by phantom coaches. These were not so much manifestations of the world beyond as masterpieces of fake and brain-washing by the moonshine fraternity. With variations as to headlessness or otherwise of coachman and horses, and even as to coachie's sex, they scared the peasantry off the road, so that they saw nothing, and so had nothing to tell, when cartloads and horse or mule trains of crates and casks and ankers of contraband were on the move from the coast. Trewornan bridge, anciently constructed like the Wadebridge of sufficient width for a carriage, was a favoured spot for the appearance of such an apparition. Sightings of the Trewornan coach were often reported and amplified by the 'free-traders' in great-great-grandfather's time. Imagine the consternation of the Wadebridge constabulary, therefore, when quite recently an irate motorist telephoned the police station that a lumbering horse-drawn stage-coach-sort-of-thing was blocking Trewornan bridge and would not let him pass!

Old Cornwall is forever breaking through the crust!

CHAPTER THREE

SHIPWRECK AND MERMAIDS

The 'West Briton' newspaper of 9th October 1879 reports the reopening of Bedruthan Steps for public use. The previous year the unremitting battering of the sea had undermined the steps and carried away the lower section. Bedruthan is one of a chain of bays from Trevose Head to Newquay (then little more than a cluster of cottages round the new quay at Lower St. Columb) where yellow sands are backed by huge cliffs the whole seven miles of coastline, and snarled all along with those jags of rock of every shape and size which look so splendid in the picture postcards. Down the cliff steps and zigzag paths had been hewn, obviously with prodigious effort and slight concern for life and limb, for speedy access to the beach and to manhandle wreckage and contraband up to the top for dispersal beyond the purview of the authorities. These were the Steps which gave the place its name.

In 1849, a generation earlier, a Mr. Drew of Camborne had cut an incline along the rock face above the beach, and it was this that had washed away and had been restored. Mr. Drew may well have been spurred to construct his ramp because of a shipwreck that had lately occurred there and the rampage on the beach which followed. October as often as not finds Cornwall at its freshest and sweetest. Autumnal gales blow up indeed, as the tally of shipwrecks shows; but they can be followed, like a 'transformation' scene on the pantomime stage, by the loveliest of days. Such a day was 23rd October 1846, after a night of fiendish fury. Daybreak revealed a horrifying, yet to the parishes of the north coast a magnificent sight. For the coastwise denizens of the ancient Hundred of Pydar, in which this horror-happy vision occurred, were faring as badly as anyone anywhere in that decade known as the 'hungry forties', while the season's fishing had been a failure and the harvest poor.

But now the knot of early risers staring down over Bedruthan Steps could hardly believe their eyes, that so much could have happened while they lay abed, and they not know of it. Bolts of gaily printed cottons and linens stretched unrolled along the beach as if on the counter of a titanic draper's. Muslins, calicoes, silks fluttered from the top of each rock, or with shirts and shifts were plastered wetly among the limpets and the black mussel-clusters. Cloth of every colour, every kind had piled into tangled heaps. Bales of clothes, many quite 'a la mode', had burst apart on the yellow sands or in the pools, to disclose sartorial extravagancies beyond the imaginings of simple countrywomen and their inelegant spouses. Crates, sea chests, kegs and casks of provisions for a voyage just begun punctuated a massive litter of planks and timbers, which surged back and forth in the sparkling surf the whole length of the tideline, or hitched into the jumble on the beach. The tang of tar pervaded the morning. And embedded in the sand beside what was to be named thereafter the 'Samaritan Rock', keel, bilges and splayed ribs were all that was left of the brig 'Samaritan.'

'Samaritan' was a new, well-found 220 tonner, outward bound from Liverpool for Constantinople with the yield of the looms of Lancashire. On passing through St. George's Channel into that reach of Atlantic Ocean we speak of today as the Celtic Sea, the brig ran into a hurricane. It is as certain as conjecture can be, so little evidence having survived the night, that the Master, Captain Thomas Davies, had run for shelter at Padstow. Padstow is the sole harbour of refuge in the hundred miles or so of rugged cliff, terrifying when alee, from Barnstaple to St. Ives Bay. Wreck upon wreck when ships scuttled for safety past the wrong, west side of Trevose Head had proved the need for a lighthouse there; the "red flash every 5 seconds (so reads the chart), 240 feet above sea level, visibility 20 miles" was still a year away when 'Samaritan' met her doom.

The 'Royal Cornwall Gazette' reported that on that balmy morning following the wreck the parishes of Mawgan Porth, St. Eval and even as far afield as St. Merryn were emptying onto the scene of the disaster. The Cornish were great walkers. Miners, who would walk miles to the pithead, climb down a thousand feet of ladders, toil the whole shift without a single mechanical aid, climb back to surface and walk home, were ever foremost among the wreckers. But in the race to the wreck no one, neither fisherman nor farmhand nor their womenfolk, was far behind. While a sentence in the 'Gazette', "it was lamentable that there should be found amongst these miserable wretches (the 'Gazette' was on the side of the landlords!) men who would stand up in the pulpit to preach the word of God," indicates the extent to which the populace was addicted to wrecking.

For three riotous days the people of the local parishes converged on Bedruthan Steps, scuffled down brandishing crowbars and axes, the tools of their trade - not that with the loot so spread out for the taking there was much to dislodge or dismember - and happily burdened clambered up again. A contemporary verse sums it up:-

> "The Good Samaritan came ashore,
> To feed the hungry and clothe the poor.
> With barrels of beef and bales of linen,
> No poor soul shall want for a shilling."

Such licence was not to be condoned. The excise officers, lacking that military support which had sometimes been available during the wars, could do little to stem the wrecking on the beach. Afterwards they searched practically every house around, recovering some of the spoil and making arrests by the dozen, so that Bodmin gaol was half full, it was said, of St.

Bedruthan Steps, where the Samaritan came to grief 1846. Courtesy Mrs. D. Nicholls.

Eval men. But threat even of transportation was no check to the busy, quarrelsome, triumphant to-do at Bedruthan. Most of the looters got away with their plunder, often by subterfuge. A farmer hides an anker of brandy under his wife's bed, then in collusion with the family doctor deters the officers by affirming she is in labour. A gatepost is hauled out of its socket as an exciseman rides into view, a keg is transferred from shoulder to hole, the post is planted back on top of it. The kitchen dresser is dragged in front of a cupboard stuffed with clothes from the wreck, and the officers search in vain. Few homes but kept their treasures, however the lawmen probed! A like resourcefulness was evidenced seventy and ninety-odd years on when U-boats were in action off the coast and cargo drifted in.

Long after the 'Samaritan affair silk dresses and every sort of finery and 'trinkaments', some cherished as heirlooms, were worn about the neighbourhood. Other prizes were preserved in other ways. There was the case of the partners Northcott and Lee who found some gold coins and agreed to 'split.' Mounting the Steps they spotted a 'Preventive' at the top. At an anxious council of war it was agreed that Northcott should hand over his share to Lee while Northcott made his way home. There, when the coast was clear, Lee would join him for sharing out. Hours later, when Northcott was doubting the loyalties of friendship, Lee turned up muddy and dishevelled. He had been robbed. All the village noted that not long afterwards George Lee bought a cottage and the adjoining meadow.

Sometimes the ebb tide, scouring out more sand than its wont from Bedruthan Bay, reveals the keel of the 'Samaritan', hard by the fatal rock which bears her name. I wonder what became of the two survivors, who escaped the fate of their nine shipmates and got away over that very rock when their ship struck between sundown on the 22nd and sunrise on the 23rd October 1846.

THE BALLAD OF THE SAMARITAN

Land wars with Sea, mindless of ships and men.
These elvan fangs North Cornwall bares repel
Atlantic blasts never more wild than when,
Brewed of a night black as the Earl of Hell,

The clash of Titans caught 'Samaritan',
Terrible at midnight tore her wide,
Prodigious as if Earth again began
To heave her mountains through primordial tide.

Then truce, an inch here gained, surrendered there;
Calm off Bedruthan, ships proud-plumaged sail:
Where gloomed Land's 'hungry forties', want and care
That night dispelled, A storm and sunshine tale!

'Samaritan' left Mersey, laden low -
Manchester prints for Byzantine bazaar,
Silks for Sultana and Seraglio,
Preston linens, Liverpool-shipped for far

Exotic, beckoning Constantinople.
Soon, provisions casked, cloth, clothes in bales
Stowed tight below, through late October's opal
Morning she ghosts past haze-hid peaks of Wales.

Breeze freshens, backs to north'ard, the Irish Sea
Shivers awake and gallops his white horses,
The rigging, whistling, conjures up cumuli.
"All hands to reef to'gallants, furl the courses!"

Pembroke's to port now, rainbows toss in spray,
The foc's'l's merry - eastern prospects thrill!
But Captain Davies in unsure dismay
Ponders the weather glass; it's falling still.

Now to her tops'ls clinging topmen trim
The brig: she skitters like a shag before
The young gale gusting. Helmsmen sou'westered, grim,
Feet straddled, fight the rudder lest she yaw.

The storm is westering. Up with the helm!
They'll raise Trevose and fly for Padstow's lee:
No heaving-to, lest waves abeam o'erwhelm -
They dare not wear the brig to meet the sea.

Dusk. At stupendous crests they stare. Squalls scream,
Eddy the scud that blots land's looked-for loom,
The goosewinged tops'ls burst and in pennants stream,
'Samaritan' grinds and labours through the gloom.

Dark. Is it east or west Trevose they speed?
No lighthouse warns. Waves on the taffrail thunder
Sweeping the poop; lost helmsmen's cries recede.
"Let go both bowers!" She broaches, gunnels under.

Masts crack, slow crumple outboard; stays whip-lashing
Tug at the hull scupper to scupper rolled,
Unstable, like a log awash. Seas smashing
Hatches and companion, flood the hold.

Gone - boat and deckhouse, captain, hands and bos'un,
Chippie and mate from pitching foredeck, who
Slipped the bow anchors. So consuming Ocean,
Naming his own calls nine, and leaves but two -

Two drenched, spray slashed, fright stiffened, lashed to the wreck,
Who watch, already half-ghosts hovering then,
Themselves retch, gasp and bend submissive neck
To Atlantic, merciless to ships and men.

Puppets jerking in a giddy arc
They see, sixth-sensed, nor moon nor starshine lit,
The cliff form substance out of screaming dark,
Feel drag and crash, hear the brig groan and split.

They live, these two; cut free, down the counter tumble,
Touch ground glim-streaked with undertow's withdrawing,
Knee-deep evade a breaker's clutch, cling, stumble
Bleeding to safety, up the cliff face clawing.

....

One word - Wreck! - wings the wind. Dawn falsely smiling
Shows of 'Samaritan' scarce semblance left;
Gear, planks adrift or, tar- and sand-stuck, piling
Along the foreshore; beach, each pool and cleft

Free Fair that day for goods burst bales spill forth.
Through furze and heath and down the Steps they swarm -
St. Merryn folk, St. Eval, Mawgan Porth,
They flock from mine and haven, hamlet and farm.

Look! Linen shirts for men, shifts, shawls for maids;
Long bolts of cloth a-tangle; floral printed
Cotton frocks, silk fashions, ribbons, braids,
Caps, lace! Cry Harvest Home, God's gifts unstinted!

Law, Duchy rights - who cares? There's beef for dinner,
Timber to build a porch or mend a frame!
Men, women, fisherman, farmhand, preacher, tinner -
All grab and bundle, shout and shove the same!

The breakers roll on Cornwall's bastioned shore,
Stout vessels perish still, brave seamen drown,
But never shipwreck won for wreckers more
Than when the good 'Samaritan' went down.

One quiet summer's evening nearly twenty years before the 'Samaritan' laid her bones with all the other skeletons of lost ships on the hungry sands, a spectacle far more frightening to the 'locals', and far less satisfying, was witnessed at Mawgan Porth. It was discussed so widely that news of it was reported in the 'West Briton' newspaper of 6th July 1827, and again in a subsequent issue.

A young fisherman who lived on the shore at Mawgan Porth had walked across the beach when the tide was out, to meet a neighbour. The shreds of day hung in the west; they would fish together for sprats while there was still light to see. Approaching a point which bounded the cove he heard a voice calling - a queer, cracked voice which, coming as it did from a cave, must be the voice of his friend distorted by echoes. This cave, accessible only at low water, had two outlets. Through one the sea flowed even at the lowest ebb. Into the other, which was above beach level, the youth climbed to seek the caller in its dim depths. He saw the jet pools within, darker than the rocks they mirrored save when the entering tide shook loose the ripples, but not his partner.

Someone, though, something, was in the cave. And there, on a boulder before him as his eyes adjusted to the darkness, appeared a shape. A shape of human form glaring at him through a mane of hair. The devil himself! The young man skidded down over the seaweed to the sand and fled home with the fear of the fiend in his heels.

But the apparition was not Old Nick. Three of these creatures appeared to watchers on the cliff next morning, and the day after five, in full daylight; visitations which threw the whole neighbourhood into such a turmoil that the opinion of the 'West Briton' reporter - now there was a man who knew his onions! - was listened to with bated breath and afterwards read, by such as had the art, with misgivings. Mermaids! That's what they were. Mermaids.

Talk of mermaids was common in Old Cornwall; not kindly talk at that. And nowhere was belief in their sinister powers stronger than on this northern coast. For everybody knew how the Doombar at Padstow had come about, and what a toll it had taken, by 1827, of good ships and good men. At some time in the past a Padstow archer had mistaken a mermaid for a fish, and shot her. As she lay dying on the reef in the Camel estuary, transfixed by that luckless arrow, she cursed the town and summoned the sand to choke the harbour entrance.

It has to be admitted that the Mawgan Porth mermaids must have been of a less attractive breed than she who lured Matthew Trewhella down to the depths at Zennor Cove or that other siren who drowned young Lutey off Cury. This news scoop of the month related how the larger mermaids, sleeping face down on a rock beneath the watchers, were human from the waist up, their bodies coloured "exactly like that of a Christian." Their arms, though, were as short as fins. Their lower parts were bluish and ended in a tail. Their hair was over nine feet long. As they slept the swell would wash over them, and receding leave them dry again, while the younger mermaids swam and dived around them. The spectators could make so convincing a report because they were no more than forty feet above, which enabled them to throw accurate stones at the lazing adults for almost an hour: a risky exercise, you might think, bearing in mind the Doombar. But it seems that the stones were ignored.

Seals? Not so - mermaids!

Now you know! But perhaps a cub reporter of 1827, with a column to fill, was not so cognizant of the feminine form as his modern counterpart. Or would you insist that witnesses see only what they expect to see? It's little green men today. Yet what with pisceys and spriggans and the 'knockers of the mines', hasn't it always been?

Mermaids, or merrymaids as the Cornish called them, are not heard of nowadays, except for the one carved into a pew for all to see in Zennor parish church. Shoreside enchantresses have been storied throughout history, from the sirens who lured sailors to destruction when Ulysses took the long way home from the siege of Troy, to the "fair pretty maid" of the sea-chanty "with a comb and a glass in her hand." Not all mermaids sported fish tails. Ulysses' sirens, who chanted those alluring songs which sent a helmsman so crazy with desire that, unless he had stuffed up his ears with wax, he would steer straight for the rocks they sang from, were glamour-girl-headed birds deprived of their wing feathers for having lost a Song for Europe contest with the sacred Muses. Other mermaids managed so well ashore that they must have had legs. You could mistake them for mere mortals; they were the more dangerous for that. But the mermaids were never more dangerous than when they adopted human babies, and took them under their protection. You met a girl at the seaside..... and you were in trouble! Like Walter Trewoofe at Perranporth.

Perranporth, noted over a hundred years ago as "a promising little watering place" and today well exceeding expectations, is that boundary of Perranzabuloe parish which confronts, wrote an ancient historian, "a very troublesome neighbour, the tempestuous ocean." Long before Victorian ladies with their parasols and big busts and bigger bustles swept the

Perranporth - 'Ware Mermaids!' Courtesy David Clarke.

holiday sands with their voluminous skirts, while 'mashers' in straw boaters and peppermint rock blazers skimmed 'ducks and drakes' into the curling surf, a farm labourer named Pennaluna - Penna the Proud - so attracted the notice of the local squire by his industry and honesty that Squire made him manager of one of his farms in the parish. This promotion, and a general antipathy against a man who worked so hard, and was so patently better than everybody else, aroused the envy of the village and would have aroused gossip too, had he ever done anything to gossip about.

Honor Pennaluna had been the village beauty, and marrying the irreproachable Penna had forfeited the friendship of all the young men around, having never enjoyed that of the women since leaving her childhood behind. Loneliness, her man being so busy from dawn to dusk, led her often to the beach, where nature is so busy about you that you are never alone. But this the neighbours did not understand. And their tongues wagged the louder when she took her daughter Selina with her as soon as the child could toddle.

Selina had been a different baby, in a strange sort of way, from other babies in the parish, and even more distinctive as a child. She developed into a young woman of startling beauty, but with a detached manner and blank expression which betokened the simple mind - or something more sinister by far. It shocked the neighbourhood that she and her mother had bathed together ever since her infancy, and Selina was singularly at home in the water. When she was bobbing about among the waves folk saw in her - and you may be sure there were many around to look - an animation never observed at other times. For sure Selina was a changeling - a fairy's or more likely a mermaid's child! How else would she so safely ride the breakers which rolled in on Perran sands?

By the time she was eighteen her companion on the beach was no longer her mother but, when his work allowed, her father. Penna found relief in the quiet company of his daughter from the tongue of his wife. For good wife though she was, Honor disapproved - and said so at every opportunity - of her husband's humility under the taunting of Tom Chennals, the 'hind' or bailiff of Squire's scattered farms.

Chennals had once aspired to the hand of the lovely Honor, who had turned him down for Pennaluna, whereupon the hind did his utmost to make their lives a misery. He carried tales to the Squire and found fault with Penna's work, though to little avail, for the Squire recognised a good man when he saw one. These accusations, however, did not turn him against Chennals either, the fellow being a sound farmer who knew his job.

One fateful day Walter Trewoofe, Squire's nephew, turned up at the manor house; a handsome, dashing soldier sent to Cornwall by a regimental surgeon with advanced views, for sea-bathing to heal wounds sustained in the French war. The young officer met eighteen-year-old

Selina and her father on the beach, and could not get her out of his mind. He admitted as much to Tom Chennals, his guide to all the likeliest spots for hunting, fishing and shooting, who perceived at once how to hit the Pennalunas where it hurt. Selina's demureness, he told the soldier, was only a mask. Beneath that guileless exterior the girl was a hussy, ripe for the plucking - an assessment with which the envious villagers readily concurred when supping a mug of ale, or a noggin of moonshine, maybe, at young master's expense at one of the several Perran kiddleywinks. So Walter Trewoofe had no doubts as to how to speed his convalescence.

To further this project Chennals visited one of Squire's farms far off in Penwith, threw out the tenant for drunkenness, and then persuaded his master to send Penna there to put the place in order for the man's successor. With the father reluctantly out of the way Walter Trewoofe then introduced himself to the mother. Honor was flattered by the attentions of the gentry both to herself and to her daughter. Soon the young couple were walking the beach together, even swimming together to the delighted scandal of the parish, and idling in the sun among the dunes as couples do, it is said, to this very day.

The leaves began to fall, and the winds blew chilling from the wild north west, and cured and contented Mr. Trewoofe rode back across the Tamar to rejoin his regiment. But it was a saddened Pennaluna who came home to find his happy companionship with Selina ended. She became morose and even further withdrawn, her beauty faded with the leaves, and everybody could see the girl was ailing, and knew why. Taunted by Chennals about his daughter's condition Penna felled him with a blow to the jaw, and was sacked by the Squire. To the misery of dismissal was soon added the ignomony of the birth of Selina's base-born son, and the grief of her death. They buried her in the churchyard among the sands she had loved. Still, the death in child-birth of an unwed village wench, with her bastard but one more tribute to the virility of gentlefolk, was no novelty then.

Gossip overflowed awhile, then fastened on other topics. The Pennalunas had ventured above their station and been humbled to everyone else's satisfaction, for few approve of success unless it be their own, and there was nothing more to be said. The Pennalunas picked themselves up and struggled and thrived; misfortune cannot long put down such honest endeavour as theirs. And the couple would walk, together now, along the lonely beach, each with separate memories of their lovely girl, and somehow she would seem near to them again.

Years passed. Walter Trewoofe after a dissolute life in London resigned his commission and returned to Cornwall, his uncle's heir. With Tom Chennals, though, everything went amiss. His crops failed, his cattle died, his horses broke their knees and his ricks caught fire. In despair he took to the bottle. Then he, too, was dismissed from his farm. However, with his friend Walter Trewoofe's help he rented a cottage on the cliff, and there the village reprobates gathered for carousals such as Perranzabuloe had never known before.

One night, after a particularly wild party at Chennal's, Mr. Trewoofe took a wrong path and found himself on the beach at midnight. About to retrace his steps, he heard a woman singing. It was the most exquisite music he had ever heard. It came from an archway of rocks which, submerged at high tide, now at low water reared black and monstrous against moonlit sands. He followed the voice down across the wet, glinting beach till all at once he found himself approaching, under the archway, a young woman of ravishing beauty. She screamed and made to flee back into the dark recesses behind her, but he seized her arm. She turned towards him, recognised him at once for all that ill-living had staled his once handsome features, and looked lovingly at him. Her face became the face of Selina, pale, strangely glowing, inexpressibly lovely. He gazed into her eyes, enraptured. There was a power in her glance that he had never known while she lived. He could not move......

The flooding tide was lapping his feet when he awoke from his trance. He was alone. He shouted her name; "Selina! Selina!" But the echo of his voice was all he heard - that and the wavelets gurgling into the rock pools. He waded to the tidemark, stopping now and then as the sound of the sea seemed very much like laughter, and at last got home.

Thereafter Selina filled his mind, however little he had thought of her before. He would stray down to the beach and sit there sorrowing. An old fisherman, who lived on the shore in an upturned boat and watched the belated mourner's every step, saw on such occasions 'merrymaids' riding the white horses; and Mr. Trewoofe's wanderings became the talk of the parish - which of course is how this story came to be told. It was said that Trewoofe saw the mermaids too. The local priest deemed it his duty to seek out the distracted gentleman as he loitered among the rocks, and heard from Walter's own lips the whole story. Not to worry! counselled the holy man. Fantasies! Lay off the drink and they'd disappear.

Walter Trewoofe avoided the cottage on the cliff for a few days, but soon he was back again. This time, though, as he was about to tip back his tot and then join in the dancing (the pious in Cornwall always mentioned drinking and dancing in the same breath!) some invisible power checked him. He paled and seemed about to faint, and so it was for several nights on. To his uncle's concern he went into a decline. Physicians were no help to him. The villagers all knew what the trouble was; although they said that Mr. Trewoofe had been ill-wished, and by whom else but by the Pennalunas and their bastard grandson? they guessed the truth. An impluse to visit yet again the cave where he had seen the maiden he had loved and forsaken was now countered by a dread of the place, from which you may judge that the fellow was being driven by those warring elements of remorse and desire to the verge of insanity.

But love, early abused, mystically revived, would not be denied. Well enough to join once more in the roistering at Chennal's cottage, one dark night Walter found his footsteps taking him down the cliff path rather than home to the manor. The tide was at the ebb, and eagerly he hurried over the starlit sands. Hark! He was not disappointed - it was the same glorious voice, this time in joyful song. And did he hear other voices in chorus? Surely not; they were echoes from the creviced cliff. As he reached the rocks the singing stopped, and his footsteps with it. He was suddenly aware that the breeze was freshening and chill. What was he doing, down there on the beach at night? He turned to retreat. But a fresh outburst of song checked him. Now it was sad, utterly compelling. The words rang clear; "Our sweet earth-child died this day."

Of course, the anniversary of Selina's death! The singing drew him on, powerless to retreat. He rounded the rocks and came to the archway there. As abruptly as before the singing ceased, to be replaced by an appalling burst of laughter from the recesses within. And at its mouth, dim yet unmistakeable in the starlight, sat Selina.

"You did not always come so slowly to your loved one", she said, extending her arms. Enraptured, every doubt dispelled, Walter flung himself into her embrace, clasped her, buried his face in her breast. Selina!...... but cold, so cold. Delight gave place to dread. Selina's face, Selina's voice, but not Selina's shape! A mermaid's shape! He struggled to break away, but was held as in a vice. She kissed him full on the lips. No mortal's kiss, lasting but the hour, she told him; a mermaid's kiss, which made him hers till death.

Gusts buffetted the night, stars not yet hidden by the mounting clouds glinted in the wave crests. Breakers pounded the beach, each advancing a fathom closer, withdrawing a fathom less, than the breaker before. Walter Trewoofe desperately summoned up his soldier's skills to win free, but to no avail. He implored his relentless captor to loose her hold. As well beg of the sea. Hers till death!

The gusts became continuous, grew to a gale. Spray slashed the terrified victim, his cries lost in the roaring of the sea, and glistened on the avenger's scaly skin. Not spray now but water slopped up to his ankles, covered his knees, swirled around his shrinking body. The mermaid lifted him to the rock above, and then to a higher, until she sat clasping him on the highest summit of all while the gale howled and the waves surged about them. Walter was half dead already, his doom reaching reaching up to get him. He could see, black against a rift in the cloud-wrack, the cottage he had left - how many hours was it ago? All within would be asleep, with never a thought for him. A flash amid the rolling thunder lit the place up, stark and evil. The thatch burst into flame. He saw his comrades and their doxies stumble out into the rain and wind. He saw a second flash strike

Tom Chennals, watched him pitch over the cliff edge from blinding light into darkness. Himself, he could not die. The struggle was past enduring, yet he could not die, not until the utmost measure of atonement had been wrung from prolonged agony.

Villagers gathering on the shore, awake as always to the chance of a wreck, watched Walter Trewoofe in the dawn twilight clinging to the one rock above the mermaid's cave that was not yet submerged.

"How don't 'e cast off and swim ashore?" someone asked. "Tide 'll carry 'un in."

"Cain't. Merrymaid 'ave got 'un. I seen she holding 'un back."

"Giss'long, tweren't nothing but the sea breaking!"

"'Twere she, I tell 'ee, eye for eye, tooth for tooth, for what 'e done to the merrymaid's child."

The waves surged right over the rock, sweeping him clear and bearing him seaward.

"Against the tide! 'Tedn' nature, is it?"

"Merrymaids is nature."

Bursts of laughter rode the dying wind. The stunned onlookers glimpsed waving tresses, white faces, white breasts and flashing arms which tossed Walter Trewoofe from one wave crest to the next as a new day gilded the sea. His body was never recovered, to bear to the family vault or to lay beside Selina in the graveyard on the shore.

An old, old tale of envy and spite and betrayal, but with a Cornish twist, mermaids haunting the coast in days gone by as the occasional sea monster or friendly dolphin does now! As to how the mermaid's fatal embrace came to be recorded, you must seek the answer in the clairvoyance or imagination of the professional story tellers who once strolled from village to village with their tales. The mermaid's revenge is told, one way or another, of various places in Cornwall. This follows the version of Professor Hunt (in his "Popular Romances of the West of England"), who favours St. Piran's parish on the sands - Perranzabuloe. As with faces in the fire and castles in the clouds, you can see anything in the tumbling waves if you stare hard enough (which was a problem when on look-out for a U-boat's periscope during the war). There have been no mermaid sightings for quite a while. But keep looking!

CHAPTER FOUR

"BESIDE THE SEASIDE"

Cornwall in the 'twenties' saw much of Prince Charming. A slight, handsome young man, he bustled about as often as not in a Fair Isle pullover of kaleidoscopic pattern and 'plus fours', those baggy breeches which vied with 'Oxford bags' for the favour of the rising generation (men only, skirts being 'de rigueur' for women for years to come, and none the worse for that!). And his smile did you good. When not in view he still beamed at you from chocolate box lids and the silver, silent screen. Edward Prince of Wales, no less, and more importantly to Cornishmen, Duke of Cornwall.

Prince Edward was delightfully at ease in the county which Sir Arthur Quiller Couch had already designated "the Delectable Duchy", and he put Newquay on the map as surely as his Georgian Great-Great-Uncle had publicised Brighton. Though less ostentatiously as befitted the England of King George V, while not having to assume the functions of Regent he did not bring the court with him. Nevertheless a sizeable retinue motored, or more commonly entrained, sou'westward. The Headland Hotel, conveniently adjoining the golf links, became his holiday home while Newquay received the accolade of fashion which preceded today's popularity rating. Later on the Prince turned his attention to Carlyon Bay, on the opposite side of his duchy. But all too soon kingship, of which we Cornish had such high hopes, and then a romantic attachment of which Church and State disapproved, drove him from our ken.

I first saw H.R.H. in 1920, at Truro, when less than a couple of years from the Western Front himself he unveiled the War Memorial in Boscawen Street. The bronze soldier could have been the Prince in person stepped up onto the granite plinth, or so I thought as, one of the least of the warriors of Truro College (now School) Cadet Corps, and clutching my cavalry carbine - a rifle was too massive for the likes of me - I stood at attention while the bugles sounded and the tears for other boys' dads trickled unsmudged, such was discipline, down my cheeks. Then jollifications at the County Show nearby, opened by Prince Edward, where I joined fellow juniors for a ducal handshake and then a dash ahead to wriggle through the throng for a second helping.

Edward meant a lot to his duchy, and it to him. A word from the royal lips worked wonders. Thus when visiting a South American silver mine on his world trip with his brother, George VI-to-be, he remarked that a Cornish firm - it was Holman's of Camborne - was worth a contract. Orders crossed the Atlantic. They still do. Somewhat apocryphal is the story that our Duke, on being shown the Niagara Falls, solemnly agreed with his host that there was nothing like it in England, but assured him that he could probably find a couple of plumbers in his duchy who would fix it!

But it was Newquay for sea air and ducal golf. The comparison with Brighton, though, was not entirely apt. Newquay was already on the move when the Prince diverted his youthful enthusiasms from war to peace, and was long strides ahead of the "New quay, Lower St. Columb" referred to by a reporter in 1830.

This new quay is far older than you might think. It is not the present harbour where you park above the yachts and a fishing boat or two, but seaward of that. And there are relics of another ancient pier on Fistral Bay. Whereas Crantock, at the mouth of the River Gannel, had been a port of consequence in the Middle Ages but had declined due to that plague of the North Cornish coast, silting sands, its insignificant contemporary in the lee of the headland survived to become rich and famous. The handful of fishermen's huts there was then known as Trerew Blystra, later Towan Blustry - hardly appropriate for Cornwall's premier seaside resort half a millennium after. However the naming problem was solved by the new quay built there when saintly but ineffectual Henry VI ruled.

In those days even a poor fishing hamlet might undertake major works as it no way could today. Labour could be paid for by forgiveness of sin. In 1439 Bishop Lacy of Exeter granted indulgences - pardons - to all who toiled to build the new quay. There seems to be some doubt, however, as to whether local labourers took full advantage of these credits in the Hereafter and completed the job. A hundred and sixty years on the Elizabethan historian Richard Carew was to write of "New Quay...... so called because in former times the neighbours attempted to supply the defect of nature by art, in making there a quay for the road of shipping; which conceit they still retain, though want of means in themselves or the place have left the effect 'in nubibus' (= in the clouds), and only lent them the benefit of lestercocks (= drift nets worked from the shore) and fisherboats." In 1615 there was an application to erect a pier, while it is heartening to know that four hundred years after the earliest venture, the South Pier was declared finished.

Miss S.T. Husband tells us in her book 'Old Newquay' that by the early nineteenth century there were five hundred inhabitants occupying 192 houses, twenty of them thatched. The rest would have been roofed with Delabole slate, 'broomshanked' with a cement wash, that was as significant a part of coastwise Cornwall as granite and greenstone and cob. These five hundred villagers supplemented the meagre harvest of their fields and their "lestercocks and fisherboats" by lead mining. Boys and girls commonly employed at Cornish mines, and probably their parents too, must have thought hard before taking a job at Lenhenver mine on Marty's Hill. It had been there that dumbfounded onlookers watched Mark Cardell cut his throat, walk down the hill, cross a field, and disappear over the cliff. It was supposed that poor Marty haunted the site of his spectacular exit. Few went there save of necessity.

As the century progressed the harbour began to look as we know it now. Boats were built there. Newquay men owned and captained a dozen schooners. Their principal cargoes were iron ore from the Perran mines, grain and pilchards in season, and china clay. Lead is not mentioned, which makes you doubt the profitability of the local mines. They returned with coal, guano and bone manure, limestone, and salt for fish curing. The village, growing to township around its Commercial Square, and with its Red Lion inn there long established, was active if not affluent. The pilchard shoals which from time to time filled this bay or that along the Cornish coast can have brought Newquay no such fortunes as at St. Ives, with its long established Mediterranean trade. Newquay chiefly depended on its traditional occupations, farming and fishing.

And smuggling. By 1800 the Revenue had found it necessary to station two officers at Newquay and two more at Kelsey Common, while 'cuttersmen' manned a Revenue cutter on patrol. To counter this the fishermen of Newquay, Crantock and Kelsey formed themselves into a secret society, passwords, fictitious names and all. They laid their plans at Treago farm and, when a 'run' was in the vicinity, hid the haul there prior to transporting it inland across Trevemper bridge. The main road swings you past it as you reach Newquay along the boating ponds. Two files of six horses, tied nose to tail and with one driver to a file, would plod through the night across the narrow bridge, each horse carrying a barrel slung pannier-wise on either flank, with perhaps a pyramid of kegs and bales on top. Leader horses have been told of so adept that they regularly led their train to the rendezvous on their own.

Treago was of great antiquity, formerly the manor house of the Treago's, who had built the south aisle of Crantock church. The family becoming extinct in the male line shortly after the erection of the new quay, Treago passed to a succession of owners who, as with so many of the small manor houses of the county, reduced its petty grandeurs to the practicalities of husbandry. And now, as the young nineteenth century moved out of war and the British government could turn its attention to the smuggling which so severely depleted its income, the ancient house was the headquarters of the as yet undefeated 'free traders.'

Of course the excisemen knew it, and maintained routine patrols in the neighbourhood - a routine which the smugglers took account of when about their business. The shore parties maintained with their mates afloat the closest contact possible in those days before long-range communication had moved out of the realms of fairy tale. But on one 'safe' night when the smuggling vessel came home from Ireland and covertly displayed her 'Will'o'the wisp' light (as Miss Husband described it) in Crantock bay, the two Kelsey excisemen were waiting. Some Judas had tipped the wink. However the shore party had its informers too. Four of its men hid by Treago gate, through which the officers would pass on their way to intercept the landing of the cargo at Crantock, and ambushed the hapless couple. They tied them back to back to the iron gate, and so yet another run was landed undetected. A passer-by released the excisemen next morning.

Old Newquay's chronicler tells us how as a girl - and a tomboy of a girl too, when you consider the restrictions of a late Victorian girlhood -she had explored many of the nooks and crannies of the smuggling days. Piper's Hole at Crantock was a passage from the beach to beneath the kitchen floor of Treago farm-house. This was partially choked with sand when she ventured along it. Secret cellars underlay the blue stone floors of Stephen Hoare's and Richard Carne's kitchen. Stone steps led from the latter below a wall to a sandpit under Carne's carpenter's shop. Timber was stacked on end to conceal the entrance. Miss Husband had also knocked on the floor near the kitchen chimney of the Albion Inn at Crantock, and heard the hollow sound of the smugglers' cellar the kitchen covered. One night when men were moving contraband at Crantock they discovered that they were being watched. So they crossed the churchyard and hid it in the belfry of the church. The officers of the law were too superstitious to follow.

The tea was first ashore at Newquay. Tea was as much in demand in humble homes as brandy was at the squire's; but at £1 a pound once it had passed through Customs, it was beyond the reach of the cottage folk. John Wesley refused to drink tea in Cornwall when he realised that more likely than not it had been smuggled; for even when after many tours he had converted the unruly Cornish into his most law-abiding followers, he still could never be sure. What a paradox that the out-of-chapel activities of the Wesleyans and Methodists have revolved round the teapot ever since! The tea was landed in barrels which were hauled up the 'tea hole' to the cliff-top. Then the brandy, gin or rum was unloaded, mostly in those neat little casks called ankers, from an old 8½ gallon measure, flattened so that a man could carry one under his arm. Often, lashing them together with the rope across his shoulders and behind his neck, he managed a couple.

With the introduction of the Coastguard service, and a wide-ranging reduction in the list of taxable imports, the smugglers eventually gave in. It had been almost as much a game, a challenge, an exhilarating risk as a means of livelihood. Lean years, a growing inclination of the pilchard shoals to try their luck further down the coast, and then Big Business came to the rescue - if not with the hearty approval of Newquay people. The energetic Silvanus Trevail F.R.I.B.A., J.P., one-time Mayor of Truro, moved in on Newquay. He was secretary, then Chairman, of the Cornish Hotel Company Ltd., founded in 1890 to launch schemes for hotels throughout the county. Each hotel became an independent

The Old Albion Inn at Crantock - Copyright Ivan Rabey.

company; so independent indeed that you can examine the founding documents of its most ambitious scheme of all yet find no mention of Cornish Hotels Co. Ltd., and must look to General Meeting notices in the press. The Atlantic Hotel, market value £20,000 at the time and considered second to none in the West of England, had been proposed for Falmouth. However the Falmouth Hotel Company objected, so the great square block of it rose above old Newquay instead and dominates the town like a baronial stronghold. It was an event viewed by the commercial fraternity with reservation and the fishermen with dislike, notwithstanding that prosperity flowed into the district once its doors were opened, and that Newquay was so impoverished that a few years previously its street lamps had been seized for debt.

Known as 'Trevail's Folly', the Atlantic Hotel nevertheless paid a good dividend in its first season; and Cornish Hotels had promoted, or were about to promote comparable hotels at St. Ives, Carbis Bay, Mullion, Coverack, Falmouth, Tintagel, Padstow, and so forth. And another at Newquay. The Headland.

The first Company Chairman, Major Mead, had declared as company policy that "unless the high class people were catered for there was very little profit in hotel keeping." The Great Western Railway brought them. The railway had reached Newquay by 1849; only the Cornwall Minerals Railway, a freight line, but it was a start. Not until thirty years later, in 1876, was a passenger service operated. It ran from one side of Cornwall to the other - Fowey to Newquay via Par. By 1896 the G.W.R. had taken over the branch line, having opened up the far West to the well-to-do from across the Tamar, and the tourist flood began to trickle into Newquay. High class these visitors might be, but the 'locals' disapproved of their holiday habits and said so. Mixed bathing indeed! Few British resorts permitted such depravity! Nevertheless the bathing machines trundled down the sands to the water's edge, and the screams of the merrymakers as the chilly wet penetrated serge bathing costumes vied with the rumble of the surf.

1897 was Newquay's year of destiny. The die was cast and the resort committed to that "vitality and vulgarity" observed by Poet Laureate John Betjeman, but also to universal and lasting appraisal "of glorious beaches, romantic caves and rocks below the villas, of great breakers on Fistral Bay, of two miles of translucent surf on shiny sand at Watergate Bay, of walks in beautiful and protected inland country round St. Columb Minor and across the Gannel." First, though, the clash as the new idea drove insensitively through the fears and prejudices and affronted pride of the local Cornish - a progress the more resented in that it was no up-country carpet-bagger, no Johnny-come-lately-gone-tomorrow who directed it, but another Cornishman, Silvanus Trevail.

Headland Hotel Company Ltd. moved into action in good heart, their intention being to create the best hotel in Britain. Their architect, Mr. Trevail, had drawn his plans, and his sketch of the future building portrayed the acme of Victorian elegance. You can see it framed today, in one of the wide corridors that has been devoted to photographs and mementoes of the Headland's early days. Trevail was one of the seven directors of the company, five others being Londoners and the sixth Mr. Conybeare of Tregullow, Scorrier. The G.W.R. Company was a large shareholder. The hotel was to be built on Little Fistral Meadow which adjoined both the lovely Fistral Beach and the Golf Links to the south west, and the Atlantic Hotel land, and below that the harbour, to the north east. This involved fencing in the site, which an embankment had enclosed the previous seventy years or so without, however, excluding the public. It is a guess that this enclosure had been carried out by a Mr. Teffrey, from whose heir the company bought the Meadow on a 996 years' lease. But the fisherfolk had from time immemorial regarded the whole promontory as common land, a convenient adjunct to the harbour for drying nets and laying out the Monday washing on rocks and furze bushes, as on St. Ives' 'Island' to this very day - out of season. And the best of spots, too, for recreation, 'tea treats' and such. Moreover their Huers' House stood up there near the edge of the cliff, where the watchers had a wide view from Towan Head to Trevelgue Head, and could be easily seen from the harbour. You can visit the Huers' House, seaward of the Atlantic Hotel: a strange little edifice like a Disney dwarfs' castle with man-sized doorways. You marvel at that romantic, suppressed genius among the fishermen, whoever he may be, who dreamed it up. From it every autumn, though not nowadays, 'huers' maintained a lookout, dawn to dusk, for the pilchard shoals that would spell contentment for the fishing community and perhaps a fortune for the few; though to be sure the shoals had been disappointing in recent years, and in '96 had not turned up at all. But the luck would surely change. Spotting the sheen of a million silver fish, the huers would again signal the harbour to launch the seine boats, and would direct them to the haul.

This was the site, as hallowed in its way as the sacred lands of the Apaches in the American West which contemporary businessmen also sought to exploit, that Silvanus Trevail and his Board of Directors were determined to appropriate. Resentment boiled over into action. The West Briton of 15th July reported that the previous Friday an auction sale of materials used for fencing-in the site had been proclaimed by the town crier of Newquay for that evening. When the crowd assembled there the auctioneer made a joke about selling the Huers' House, which with a fresh coat of whitewash looked quite lovely in the westering sunshine, and further insulted the fishermen by 'knocking it down' for less than a shilling. The following evening, at eight o'clock, the townspeople headed by the

Newquay brass band marched through the main street, up to the Headland, and removing the fencing hoisted on the Huers' House flagpole a banner bearing the arms of Cornwall and the motto "One and All." (Arms and motto are now set into the wall there). Then they returned to Red Lion square, where they stopped the Atlantic Hotel bus, on its way from the station with a load of visitors. However two policemen led the horses through the jeering mob. You may well imagine what the 'high class' holiday-makers thought! And the following day, the Cornish always turning to a 'tea-treat' for a great occasion, a public tea for the fishermen and their wives was held on the grounds now restored, as they thought, to common ownership.

Not so! On 12th August the Headland Hotel signboard, still in place, was daubed with tar. This prompted the Company to offer a £10 reward for information leading to a conviction. By the 31st a stout wooden site office was in place. It was a day of howling gale when a crowd swarmed up from the town with ropes. They secured the rope to the office and with a hundred of them heave-hoeing pulled it down. It broke into three sections, each of which they dragged to the cliff edge and toppled down into the surf, where it was splintered to matchwood.

When Mr. Trevail arrived by train a couple of days later to inspect the damage, the rowdies were awaiting him at the station. They pelted him with stones, 'tobbans' of turf, eggs and flour - anything that came to hand, and spat on him as he pushed past. But he was a courageous man and was not to be deterred. On his return from the site an even larger mob pinned him and his police escort against the station railings for an hour and a half. Twenty-two arrests followed. In court the defendants claimed that Little Fistral Meadow was common land and that Cornish Hotels Ltd., and not themselves, were the trespassers. The ringleader was fined 60 shillings and costs, four others thirty shillings and costs. A fair penalty for disturbing the peace, would you say, and a convenient dodging of the main issue? The building of the magnificent Headland Hotel began in 1898. Two hundred out-of-work miners were employed. They entered Newquay behind the biggest traction engine in the West, fitted with steam pipes to be used in an emergency against attack. Harsh measures for crowd control! But they kept the peace.

And so Trerew Blystra grew from the humblest of fishing hamlets to a village boasting its own new pier, and at last to Newquay, queen of the Cornish seaside and one of the principal holiday resorts in the kingdom. Sixty years ago, though, it was still very exclusive, with few visitors about except during the school holidays. I recall cycling from Truro to Newquay in term time that wonderful summer of 1920 - or was it '21, or '22? No matter - all summers were wonderful then! My school chum and I finished up at Holywell Bay and climbed up to the holy well. It is in a cave, you know, the walls luminously pink and damp from countless ages of water seeping through the mineral veins of Cornish rock. It was like standing in a Victorian lustre jug, but with the lustre on the inside. Then we went onto the beach for a dip - an immense stretch of golden sand silver-rimmed where it met the sea. And completely empty! Not a soul in sight.

Newquay was then very much a fishing port, for all the hotel and boarding house signboards that were beginning to spread from the sea front into side streets. Old Elizabethan Carew's "fisherboats" still counted for as much in the town's economy as the buildings did which were reaching forth into the Age of the Tourist, though I cannot say as much for his "lestercocks." At school we won a choir competition with "The Newquay Fishermen's Song." Cornwall's male voice choirs to this day coo the opening verse -

"The boats go out to the fishing ground
Over the moonlit sea......"

and in the next verse thunder -

"Sometimes the waves rise high,
The wild winds roar,
The angry breakers roll upon the rocky shore."

So it is all along the rugged north coast of Cornwall; sunshine and cloud, calm and storm, even in the summer time though in differing proportions. And always the sea, the sand and the rocks. And when you scan the tally of shipwrecks, particularly north-eastward along Watergate Bay and up to Bedruthan Steps, the record is appalling. In the mid-1800's the Newquay coastguards, stationed there as you know to prevent smuggling and so at odds with the populace, were already establishing their present, endearing image - life-savers and lookouts for vessels in distress. Between 1854 and 1859 they won three Silver Medals of the Royal National Institution for the Preservation of Life from Shipwreck.

Eighteen lifeboats were covering the long Cornish coast by the end of the nineteenth century; sturdy, heavy boats propelled by oars, and by sails when the wind was right, launched either from slipways or off cumbersome carriages hauled by men or horses across the beach. Newquay got its first lifeboat, the 'Joshua', in 1861. The town turned out to welcome her after the overland journey, and practically everyone -Newquay's population was nearing a thousand by then - paraded with the boat, on her carriage and proudly drawn by the six heftiest horses to be borrowed for the occasion, to the new lifeboat house in Fore Street. As the 'Joshua' set about her tremendous duties difficulties arose in drawing boat and carriage over the yielding sand. Some years later a slipway was built, and later still another lifeboat house, across the neck of Towan Head. The 1 in 3 gradient turned out to be too steep for hauling the boat back up the slip, so she had to be brought back from the harbour by road and an eight-horse team. When after World War I horses were unobtainable, problems arose that Newquay never resolved. The Newquay station used in succession eight boats, answered 66 calls, and saved 114 lives. A proud record!

Today's lifeboats, with their lofty superstructures and mighty engines, have taken over from the oars-and-sail boats we still picture when lifeboats come to mind, so that the Padstow, St. Ives and Sennen boats now cover the coast that seven boats once served. The Newquay station was closed down in 1934, fourteen years after the last of the old boats put to sea and rescued the crew of five from the ketch 'Philomene.' The difficulty of returning the boat to the boathouse away on Towan Head had proved insuperable. However, in 1940 the motor lifeboat 'Richard Silver Oliver' was stationed at Newquay, and kept on the harbour slipway. Until her removal in '45 she picked eight crashed airmen out of the sea and a fishing boat's crew of three. St. Mawgan airfield was along the coast. It is now Newquay airport, a civilian company sharing the runways with the R.A.F. since '77.

A fisherman and an old but remarkably spry coastguard yarned of wartime plane disasters. One heavy bomber had crashed in the sea soon after take-off from St. Mawgan, and there were no survivors. The lifeboatmen recovered several bodies, and found that every one wore a money belt containing gold coins. It was common knowledge at Newquay that the plane was on a secret mission to Europe, and that it carried gold bullion. Or so it was said. Another memory was of an American Liberator bomber which crashed at night when coming in to land. It hit the base of the cliff below St. Mawgan, at the mouth of a cave, and burst into flame. The lifeboat could not come closer than two or three hundred yards because of the heavy swell, soaring one moment and scraping the sand the next. Soldiers from a gun-site on the cliff rushed to help, but the tide was rising. Two of them were cut off by the tide, and with the American survivors were drowned. After one crash in the bay, however, all six crewmen were rescued by the Newquay lifeboat. How today's inshore rescue boats - rubber dinghies drawing only a few inches and driven by a powerful outboard engine - and the R.N. and R.A.F. helicopters would have helped!

You can forget those turbulent years, and much of the present hassle too, at Crantock on the western side of the Gannel. Crantock aims to turn its back on modern times, and makes a fair job of it. The village is a tight cluster at its centre, and many of its charming houses are thatched, as the whole village was in September, 1812, when following an exceptionally dry summer sparks from the smithy fire ignited the stacked grain harvest in a neighbouring farmyard. A gusty wind scattered the burning straw in every direction, and smithy and Mr. Johns's farmhouse and farm buildings were destroyed in one blinding blaze. The rest of Crantock was saved by spreading 'winnowing sheets' over each thatch and dousing them with water until the fire at the farm burnt itself out.

The Albion Inn, that one-time haunt of smugglers beside the lych gate of the church, seems not to bother with the twentieth century, let alone the coming twenty-first, when you look at it from outside. While the church beyond the gravestones is hardly concerned with the sixteenth. Or so you may conclude when you turn your gaze from its ancient but somewhat unprepossessing exterior and contemplate this loveliest of little churches, as it is inside. You are in fact savouring but fragments of its antique self incorporated within exquisite modern work. The holy figures on the Screen, for instance, were carved at Oberammergau in 1902. For Cromwell's ruffians had so desecrated St. Carantoc's, and knocked it about so much, that but for a Victorian vicar, Rev. George Metford Parsons, it would have been scarcely more than a 'picturesque ruin', as the present vicar, Rev. M. Hattam, says in his nice little booklet.

St. Carantoc had been yet another of those sons of Celtic kinglets who surrendered their rights of succession to enter Holy Church. Cynics maintain that they did so to avoid family squabbles and bloodshed, probably their own. Others see them as having dedicated their authority to promoting the Christianity which was erupting in the dark ages throughout the Celtic world. Carantoc had left Wales for Ireland to sit at the feet of St. Patrick. Then he crossed to Cornwall in the customary coracle. He had cast his travelling altar-stone into the sea to guide him, and instead of leading him straight down it took him across, the miracles of the saints proving far more efficacious than the magic of the heathen priests they were determined to circumvent. Carantoc's pet dove crossed to the River Gannel with him, and showed him where to found his church.

Crantock parish included Newquay until 1900. It had risen to the eminence of a priestly college, Dean, Prebendaries, Canons and all, before the Conquest, Edward the Confessor granting its charter. But by the fourteenth century it had become slack and even scandalous. The canons were letting some of their houses to laymen, who had to be excommunicated by the Bishop of Exeter before he could turn them out; others were in use as taverns, disorderly ones at that. And the Dean was bankrupt. Bishop Grandisson reorganised the college, but to slight effect. In 1412 the central tower collapsed. You would have guessed from the disparity of the two roofs that something was missing. The higher chancel had been for the clergy, the lower nave for the humble laity. The church tower was rebuilt at the western end, and as you can see has needed attention too.

Many Cornish churches were desecrated by the Roundheads, and none worse than St. Carantoc's. Nor had less been done to restore some of their former charm and beauty; Crantock was such a poor parish up to a

The Huers' House, Newquay. "They signalled the pilchard shoals to seine-boats in the bay and to the harbour below". Courtesy David Clarke.

century ago, its harbour silting up and already fallen into decay. But that fateful year for Newquay, 1897, was the year in which Rev. G.M. Parsons completed the first phase of his restoration and appealed for funds to finish the work. The whole district was becoming wealthier and much could at last be done. By 1907 St. Carantoc's was as you see it now. Miracles are still worked, but they usually take longer than when the saints came sailing in.

CHAPTER FIVE

SAINTS, SANDS AND DIGGERS

Have you ever wondered why saints you never heard of crop up in place-names all over Cornwall? Most are not Cornish at all, however they appear to be. While later, south coast saints came over from Brittany and holy men and women were shared by the two Celtic nations, the earliest on the scene were Welsh and Irish missionaries of the Celtic Church. This was the one Christian fellowship in Western Europe, when barbarians were stampeding through the Roman Empire and the Roman Church was split and struggling to survive, that had the will and the power to spread. The missionaries, a prince or two but mostly brethren of the communal hermitages of Leinster and Ulster, set out from the Emerald Isle to find in Cornwall good ground for sowing the seeds of their faith, and ground too for their own martyred bones and the age-defying sanctuaries which the faithful were to raise over them.

So long as they came singly, without threat of conquest, the saints - then ordinary people (if with a lot to say) with ordinary needs - were well received. It may be supposed that they won their martyr's crowns by provoking the local chieftains just once too often; that some of them even contrived their own glorious demise by deliberately outwearing the patience of their hosts. They disembarked on the north coast of Cornwall, sometimes from the most improbable craft. The Princess Ia floated into St. Ives Bay on a leaf, a coracle of course, and none the less remarkable a voyage for that. Piran, patron saint of Cornwall and tinners, drifted ashore at Perranporth on a millstone, which is not so simple to explain. And some came in droves, an invasion of saints. They landed at Hayle in the early sixth century, seven hundred of them, and ran into trouble.

Hayle is separated from the sea by a long, rocky ridge against which hillocks of fine white sand, growing almost mountainous nine hundred years ago, have piled into 'towans' or dunes. The ridge is the seaward arm of what had been a creek until, dammed and sluice-gated, it became Phillack Lake and latterly Hayle Pool. The ridge end which overlooks the estuary, and is now an extensive chalet and caravan park, has been called Riviere, with variations of spelling, ever since it was first documented. It commands a breath-taking view of St. Ives headland across the bay, and of enormous white-sand beaches, and of the swell creaming on the reef. But the view was not what engaged King Teudar's attention when he stood on Riviere Towans almost fifteen hundred years ago, where a Roman fort once dominated the estuary.

Teudar was a vassal of the great Cornish kingdom of Dumnonia, the eastern frontiers of which ran south from Severn to the Channel. His

Godrevy Lighthouse.

realm in the far South West had been inaccessible by land, too remote, too poor for Rome in her heyday to concern herself about either spiritually or in matters other than the shipment of tin to Gaul. The garrison of the great Roman camp at Gwithian, established to that end, had been withdrawn long before Teudar's time. Dumnonia, following the withdrawal of all the legions from Britain, had heavier problems to bother her than Teudar's. The great Arthur himself was like as not hammering at the Saxons on the Wiltshire border.

You must picture Teudar, for that is all the picture there is of him, standing like an eagle in its eyrie in front of his castle near the old Roman site on the towans. The castle was no more than a low-walled 'round' with central round-house and surrounding hutments, and he had moved into the open the better to glare down at the estuary beneath his feet, motioning back the warriors crowding behind him lest their spear points should catch the sunlight. An armada of wide-beamed, clumsy vessels was lumbering across the bar with the tide high but still flooding; not the trim pirate craft of the Saxons, but bristling with foreigners nonetheless. Wild Irish for sure, for among the boats were high-gunnelled oddities made of skins stitched and tarred and folded over timber and wicker frames; curachs stout enough for rowing and sailing "on the broad-bosomed ocean", as the Roman poet Lucan wrote of them.

Teudar was not to know that they were men of peace. Whether they were or not, however, their landing in such numbers would eat the countryside into starvation and disrupt the local economy. Nor did he know that their leader, Prince Fingar, had planned to round Lands End but had been driven into the Hayle (the word means estuary) by the weather. Fingar's expedition had set out for Armorica, later known as Brittany, and it may now have been his intention to lead it across the isthmus, Penwith then being nearly an island, and take ship from Marghadyou ('Thursday market' - Marazion) or the Mount. That was the favoured trade route when Lands End was the Cape Horn of those days. Well, mused Teudar, considering that possibility too, a fat merchantman to be unloaded and charged up to the hilt with Irish gold was one thing, a fleet crammed to the gunnels with Irishmen quite another. As Prince Fingar came ashore, King Teudar moved down the towans and attacked.

It was a one-sided conflict, not that every man of seven hundred Irishmen would have turned the other cheek. The Christian missionaries scattered throughout West Cornwall, each to set up a cell and an oratory, or even two, as St. Euny did, and plant the cross where parishes were some day to spread. There was no more thought of Armorica. Their leader was dead. They had seen him reeling down the ridge and making off inland with a gash in his neck that gave no hope of survival, and they had to stay where they were, in this hostile territory, and make of it what they could. Doubtless numbers of their followers settled with them though no parchment chronicles their humbler destiny. But many perished in the slaughter on the sands, while likely enough the boat crews shoved off to sea again and pulled away out of the annals of history too.

Legend records of Fingar that he belongs to that coterie of the faithful who, though decapitated, plod manfully on. For his head being stricken off as he led his band ashore he picked it up, carried it down the dunes and across fields and marshes destined to become Hayle town thirteen centuries afterwards, and put it down at Gwinear. There, inspired by such holiness, the local infidels accepted the cross, and buried the saint where now the church bells summon the faithful to evensong.

Through centuries of changing pronunciation Fingar has come to be known as St. Gwinear, the Irishman Erc (or Ercus), St. Erth, Gothian St. Gwithian and so forth. Fingar's sister Piala became St. Felicitas because the Normans, when they took over Phillack parish, deemed it a more appropriate name for a saint of whom they knew so little. Fingar's, Piala's and Erc's parishes contain modern Hayle, Gothian's adjoining Piala's at the eastern end of St. Ives Bay. At the western end Ia was sole patron saint of St. Ives until St. Peter and St. Andrew, no less, were enlisted to assist. Having been refused permission by Prince Fingar to join his expedition Ia had set off on her own, and got to Cornwall before him. A thousand years were to pass before a parish, St. Ives, was constituted in her name. St. Anta, her neighbour at Lelant, had half as long again to wait, even though as at St. Ives the place where she had settled (Lan-Anta - church of Anta) bore her name. Ia's princely brother St. Uny got Lelant, as it were, Anta eventually acceding to Carbis Bay, a patronage she had to share with All Saints. Anta, too, had arrived in the bay before Fingar, a jumping of the gun, so to speak, which disadvantaged her and that other wonderful woman Ia in the parochial promotions list.

They and others of that holy band we revere as the ancient saints of West Cornwall were all martyred by King Teudar, or it is claimed they were. The clerical records, which are the only records of him there are, and few of those survived the Reformation, revile him as a bloodthirsty pagan. Perhaps he was, though reports of his infamies were certainly prejudiced. But it is possible that the name Theodore, by which he was known in trans-Tamar Dumnonia, remnant of the foundering Christian Empire, marks him as a Christian too. Fanatics set on martyrdom are a problem anywhere; while with the world in turmoil, every stranger suspect, and flotillas of pre-medieval landing craft invading - well, what would you have done?

King Teudar met his end when visiting the boundaries of his realm beside the River Fal. He fell from his horse and broke his neck. St. Kea, the local saint, being blamed for ill-wishing the king ran away to Brittany. When he returned, the great Arthur had fallen in battle with his rebel nephew Modred, and Kea induced the widowed Queen Guenivere to atone for her philanderings in a convent. (But some say that the dates don't tally at all).

A century or two after the landing of the Armorican expedition, and that is the closest to precise dating you can get, Cornishmen and women were themselves pouring into the peninsula across the water. King Arthur was no more, his military organisation had disintegrated, and the Odin worshippers from North Germany were storming westward. From their kingdom of Wessex they burst through the frontiers of Dumnonia, severing the Cornish from their fellow Celts of Wales and driving them back to the Tamar, so that Devon and Cornwall ceased to be one nation and save for political expediency will never be so again. Refugees fled across the river. Many more took to their boats and joined their Celtic cousins, whose language and in part whose customs and saints they shared, in Armorica. They migrated in such profusion that they outnumbered their hosts, whereupon Armorica became the land of the Britons - Brittany, and the folk who lived there Bretons. Its two principal regions, Cornouaille and Domnonée, preserved the Cornish connection until Napoleon dropped them when reorganising France into prefectures.

The only impact the Saxon eruption made on the far West was the appearance of longships off the north coast. Whether the Saxons came to raid or to settle, once more the war horns rallied the tribes, and by the time the invaders had turned into Hayle estuary the Cornishmen were ready for them. By now ardent converts, they hurled the heathen back to his boats with gratifying slaughter, and hanged captured chiefs at the haven mouth, like shot crows in a field, to warn off the survivors and their piratical comrades.

With the Saxon monarchy established in England, and before the Danish menace claimed its undivided attention, King Egbert exacted homage from all the petty kings of Dumnonia. But the further west you go the less difference did a few Saxon thanes make to native customs and stock. Despite a transitory if triumphant progress through Cornwall by King Athelstan, Alfred the Great's magnificent grandson, about 930 A.D., and the comings and goings of Cavaliers and Roundheads, the English left most of the county to itself until the advent of the Great Western Railway. The Cornish are a mixed populace now, and are becoming a mixed race, though still short of the Indian and African strain. Yet true Cornish abound, especially in the far West. Dark haired and complexioned, a primordial Mediterranean ancestry is so marked in their features that newcomers invented in explanation a Spanish galleon wrecked in Mounts Bay with the local maidens falling for the gallant castaways. It is reckoned that your average Cornishman is two inches shorter, and two inches wider across the shoulders, than the English, so that a company of the Duke of Cornwall's Light Infantry (now combined with the Somersets) took up more space on parade than men of other regiments. How it must have worried sergeant majors, when placing their markers for a parade east of the Tamar, to have to allow for a Cornish presence!

When William the Conqueror was consolidating his stolen kingdom even to the uttermost Cornish manor, something extraordinary happened to the north coast of Cornwall; an upheaval as cataclysmic as the drowning of the land of Lyonesse, which old chronicles maintain happened at the same time. This upheaval was a 'sand blow', common enough but unprecedented as to size. Millions of tons of sand, mountains of sand, heaped up on the sands already packing the coast, to lift up over the cliffs in another blow six hundred years later, smothering the countryside well inland and choking, among other depredations, the river way to the port of St. Erth. Today the towans, white no longer save close to the beaches, have been contained within a mesh - the roots of long, reedy 'bent' or 'marram' grass, interspersed with patches of short turf which lie like velvet on the tamed sand. However towans not so planted will still 'take off' in wind and storm, as at Hayle harbour in the 1970's.

Major blows have buried ancient homesteads of every phase of development from stone to iron age - medieval houses and whole villages, a Roman camp at Newquay and two more at Gwithian, 'dark age' oratories and medieval chapels, and the church of St. Uny Lelant on the western side of the Hayle estuary. But St. Uny's was dug out at the expense of the local gentry and made good. Physical and man-made features of the landscape vanished beneath the dunes like Pompeii beneath the ashes of Vesuvius, though not so suddenly, and are only now being restored to daylight, thought provoking and mysterious, a corner at a time.

The sand can have blown only from a seabed heaved above the waves by some submarine convulsion; a reversal, could it be, of the post-glacial tilt to the north, so that now the north coast of Cornwall lifted and the south dipped? Was it then, or sooner, that the sea swallowed Mounts Bay forest? You can still see its tree trunks uncovered at the lowest of spring tides, while fragments over twice the age of the resurrected timbers of the 'Mary Rose', and darkly resisting decay, wash ashore at Praa Sands. Had a wrinkle in earth's crusty skin left old Cornwall down by the stern, where Lyonesse had sunk, and listing a little to starboard, as if her cargo had shifted? Whatever had happened, and may be happening now, albeit gradually and lacking the dash of a great occasion, sand hills piled high along the north coast. What secrets they conceal!

In the 1950's and '60's our summertime hillsides were aswarm with bare-armed and grubby youth beavering away with bricklayers' trowels in square holes and trenches, or trundling wheelbarrows along planks like apprentice tightrope walkers. Older, and even elderly, men and women with every appearance of long sojourn in the desert would emerge from portable huts with notebooks and tape measures and an aura of awesome authority to oversee the slaves. These were professors and directors of 'field studies', their acolytes the academic aspirants to such dignities, and gangs of juveniles who as incipient archaeologists performed tedious tasks, hour upon hour and day after day, that they would never have stuck at in the garden for their fathers - all for the satisfaction of unearthing a sherd, an inch of clay pipe-stem, a bone or two from an aboriginal's rabbit pie, an ox shoe, a patterned quern, a jagged fragment of flintstone to be listed as a scraper, or a change of soil texture which would fetch the magnates scrambling into the pit, thrusting aside the exultant sifter, ounce by ounce, of soil and rubble and sand and mud, who stood by glowing in the immensity of his find.

Although there is much yet to discover, clues to piece together and deductions to be made, youth does not dig there any more and the excavations dependent on their enthusiastic and unstinted labour have ceased. Can it be because there was no pay for their work? That achievement twenty years later is measurable only by cash received?

Nowhere was there greater archaeological activity than at Gwithian, where in the course of the exploration hundreds of students toiled from all over Britain. Professor Charles Thomas (who had not attained his 'chair' then) was probing a few acres of his own, as far as the National Trust and the guardians of rights of way and coastal footpaths would permit. This is not so much a tale of the coast as the tale of Cornwall in miniature. For the 'dig' revealed on that slope, and at associated sites in the vicinity, the successive elements which through the aeons have made Cornwall what it is today.

True, there was little in what came to light day by day to indicate such profundity. There was the wooden site office, around it the neatly scarred grassland and stacked 'tobbans', or turfs. White sand and darker subsoil formed geometrical patterns among the green, and muddy tracks traversed the whole. Nearer the summit you saw furze and bramble uprooted, and a more concentrated bustle of organised activity. For a week or two you could watch, in wonderment as to what it was all about, a team of experts lugging a trimmed-off tree trunk up and down. The idea was to test a theory about primitive ploughing. The result seemed to satisfy them, and a bronze age farmer might have made a better job of it. He would have needed to!

The main site of the West Cornwall Field Club's dig was at the 'T' junction where the Gwithian-Portreath road crosses a river, ketchup-red and repulsive from 'tailings' of tin mines inland, and turns sharp right, while the rough road to Godrevy runs left. It has reverted to a green and pristine nonentity, its little treasures locked away; its secrets archived. This is the story it told to those, like Charles Thomas, with "ears to hear."

Some 11,000 years ago, by the end of the last ice age with a fair proportion of the North Atlantic frozen into icebergs and ice floes, the sea level off the north Cornish coast had dropped far lower than the lowest of ebb tides today. Deeper beaches reached into the mist swirling above dwindling floes, that had drifted south from the frozen ocean and now dropped pebbles of flint which, scooped up in their glacier days, were to serve man when the land was ready to accept him. At Gwinear the river, cold and crystalline and wider than now, rippled down the valley to wind more leisurely through the sands and around dunes destitute of vegetation. There was no bar to stem the tide when it rose. At flood the valley became a tidal creek, without trace of life on its dreary banks.

Two or three thousand years nearer our own time Gwithian creek was a more hospitable nook of old Cornwall. The peninsula was gradually tilting towards the north. This and the warmer climate which released enormous volumes of ocean from the grip of the ice raised the sea level. It brought the tide further and deeper up the Red River valley. Vegetation grew lush over the land, though the towans stayed bare and shifting. There were trees in the valley, and insects, birds and animals. Wolves ravaged the river banks and deer grazed. And man arrived. He was mesolithic - Middle Stone Age - man, and where life teemed he alone was sparse. His little implements of stone and bone were disclosed at the 'dig' and further up the valley, as were places blackened by his cooking fires. His stable diet was shell fish, plucked from the rocks, but he fished too, spearing his prey in the shallows. As the glaciers receded and the climate grew milder his ancestors had moved northwards over immense periods of time, crossing the land link with France and settling in pathetic little colonies along the Cornish coast.

By 2500 B.C. New Stone Age man may have built a hut or two at Gwithian. His one sizeable settlement in Cornwall was on Carn Brea, the hill you will see some miles distant with a Norman keep at one end and a soaring modern monument at the other. These neolithic people had colonised the south coast of England, and came to Cornwall with their pottery and polished flints and primitive agriculture both overland, and from France by sea.

Bronze Age Cornwall begins a thousand years afterwards - and what time spans these are when even the Victorian era seems incredibly remote to us in our too swiftly developing days! Within six centuries it had merged into the early Iron Age. Immigrants came in waves and settled, absorbing the former occupants of the land. These ancestors of ours spoke a sort of archaic Cornish and shared the western culture of a race scattered throughout Europe. This culture takes its name from the pottery skills of people. therefore they are known as the 'Beaker' folk. A skill of greater importance lay in their rough refining of gold - ornaments of Cornish gold have been found in many parts of Cornwall, Gwithian included, this century while Sir William Lemon got a large lump of raw gold from Mylor in 1750 - and in useful and decorative working of copper and tin, and so of bronze, with the river beside the excavations reddening a little as it hurried down to the sea. Meanwhile the manufacture of efficient and quite artistic stone implements proceeded.

When Neolithic people built Stonehenge they also erected a score of smaller circles in Cornwall. Mr. F.E. Halliday considered that they were dedicated to sun worship, except in West Cornwall. The five stone circles there were temples of the Earth Goddess, a dark and sinister deity worshipped fearfully at night, as her devotees had worshipped her since the earliest times of the gods, within sound of her sometime enemy and sometime ally the Sea. You can still sense that the heaths and lichens of West Cornwall conceal the earth and stone of ancient mysteries, so will not wonder that the cult of the Earth Goddess survived in the witches of Zennor and St. Levan a few generations ago, nor that in mine silly women were still sticking pins into candle-wax dolls, while even today..... Well, old beliefs linger in these parts, and shadows strangely outlive the objects that cast them.

Meanwhile the Iron Age had dawned - and how gradual were the changes compared with those that bless, and curse, us today! Another thousand years on, and Iron Age man had a hut or two and a few tilled fields at Connor Downs, the long and ancient village (though it doesn't look it!) you drive through above Hayle on your way to Penzance or St. Ives. He may have been prospecting for tin. Vast population upheavals were erupting all over Europe. With iron replacing bronze as the dominant metal and providing the 'ultimate' weapon, the only defence was to wield it yourself. So warlike hordes which had been dispossessed of their traditional territories by tribes with prior iron-forging skills in turn dispossessed weaker neighbours. Refugees trailed along the river sides and ridgeways and crossed the Channel to conquer and settle. They were Celts, often blond, tall men. They came in tribal groups, down through the country or on the coast, built remarkable stone villages as at Chysauster, which still survives at Gulval near Penzance, and fortresses for protection against the early Cornish, and afterwards against further Iron Age invaders. St. Ives 'Island' across the bay was such a fortification. So was the summit of Trencrom hill, which dominates Hayle's western skyline. The latest Iron Age invaders arrived when Imperial Rome expanded across the Alps and into France. The legions followed them into Cornwall too, after the fighting had died down and when 'the peace of Rome' had extended so far across the Tamar that the new Cornish could leave the draughty hilltops for the convenience and shelter of valleys and of estuaries. So down they came to the Hayle River (heyl = estuary or river) and, in those days, Gwithian creek.

Professor Thomas discovered two Roman forts at Gwithian. Till then it had been thought that apart from a copied villa, a pot or two and a fistful of coins there were no signs of Roman occupation in West Cornwall. The first fort was at Godrevy, overlooking the site of the 'dig.' A medieval manor house came to light too, within its ramparts. The second was huge, all of 220 by 125 yards, with straight banks dug into the snowy sand and explaining the local name, so long used, so long a mystery, Carwin - the white fort. It lies in the Treeve Lane area, part of the embankment running through Robb Lello's boat building yard. Why it was so sited and garrisoned is but surmise: probably to protect and oversee the 'old men's workings' - the open-cast tin mines of the interior that were already reddening the river - and the shipment of the ore from the creek, along the banks of which off-duty legionaries would have dallied with the local maidens and perhaps added a further blend to the Cornish stock. There would have been another shipment too. Romans loved oysters, even had them transported post-haste overseas and up the straight highways and across the Alps to the capital, and the Gwithian oysters which, large and fat and every bit as succulent as the East Coast variety, clustered as thickly then as mussels do nowadays.

The day came when the Gwithian cohort filed aboard the galley sent to fetch them away for ever, round Lands End to Gaul. A local chieftain occupied the fort at Riviere. The white fort below was overblown, its palisade jagging up through the sand until, like the anti-Luftwaffe obstacles of 1940 that presented a stubble of posts to an airborne landing on St. Ives Bay beaches, they rotted or were removed. Dark mysteries which had survived a century or two of official Christianity were celebrated openly among the dolmens and menhirs and stone circles of the high moors. Witch doctors and priests of earth and sky, hitherto tolerated as was the Roman way, now moved as of right among the people. If the worship of the Earth Goddess and Sun and Moon had proceeded in Cornwall as elsewhere, sacrificial youths and maidens (if no captives were at hand) would have squirmed over slow druidical fires before distribution in morsels to ensure the fertility of the fields. The saints arrived none too soon.

You never knew Cunaide. Yet when you see her tombstone in the 'Plantation' at the western end of Hayle, where the main road runs straight before turning onto the causeway, you feel akin to her, as if she were yesterday's lady instead of Romano-British and laid to rest there fifteen hundred years ago. Her latin inscription, in good trim though variously interpreted because even so time has had its way, reads "Here in the grave she fell asleep, here in the grave Cunaide lies. She was thirty-three years old." Do you detect the ghost of a sob? Next to the tombstone was a grave. Both were excavated when Harvey's, the famous foundry and ship-building firm at Carnsew there, gave an ancient fort a Victorian face-lift, 1843-5, and planted it out in trees. But Cunaide - was she madam or miss? Was her death natural or did she perish in the course of the violent disintegration of the Roman Empire? Perhaps that old rascal King Teudar had a hand in it, or perhaps he mourned at her graveside - though not if she

The Plantation, Hayle c. 1880. Courtesy Royal Institute of Cornwall. Cunaide was buried here 1500 years before.

had had anything to do with the invasion of the saints. We shall never know. Yet standing before her stone you feel that she is precious to you. Yesterday's lady? Well, what are a millenium and a half in the aeons of history and prehistory at Hayle?

As you travel westward out of Hayle, with the timber yard to your right and the 'Plantation' to your left, you might think that this walled and gatewayed structure was a coastal defence mounted against a Napoleonic assault. What this masonry did conceal, however, when Henry Harvey sought to dignify that end of the town which had won him wealth and fame, were the concentric embankments of a fort. Carnsew was a headland in the estuary which in ancient times could be approached at any state of the tide, and with the mound behind it was the ideal site for fortifications, Roman and doubtless far earlier.

Nearly everything to do with Hayle is either at one end or the other - Foundry or Copperhouse nowadays. So having discussed the mysterious if lovable lady of Carnsew we are now back-tracking to her contemporary Gothian, who escaped Teudar's massacre and made his way to Gwithian, then a creek. St. Gothian's hermitage lies beneath Gwithian's still unexcavated sands. With the towans dwindling as white shell sand is transported, so much more massively than ever before, to the builders and lime-hungry farmlands of the interior, who knows what will come to light, or be shattered unregarded by automatic diggers and dumpers? More likely, though, it is buried among the foundations of the Gwithian church of about 950 A.D. This served the great Saxon manor of Connerton, established when King Egbert carved up Cornwall in the golden age of the Wessex dynasty, but with slight effect on the way of life in the far West, however it stamped the Cornish of the East. With an adjoining graveyard the remains of the Saxon church are to be found under the turf of Gwithian village's common grazing land flanking the highway. Abandoned in favour of the present thirteenth century church, it disappeared beneath the blown sand, as happened to St. Piran's oratory at Perranzabuloe. In 1808 it emerged, to be used as a cowshed until it was submerged again. It was dug out and a service conducted there in 1913, but finally vanished around 1940 "safe," says Charles Thomas, "under its blanket of sand."

A particularly spiteful act of wrecking took place near Gwithian in 1817. Wrecking, as you know, was regarded in Cornwall rather as the harvest of the sea than as crime. Like tinning, it was part of a Cornishman's way of life. The landowners jealously guarded their foreshore rights, though with no more concern for the rights of ship owners than the villagers with no rights at all, only a determination to get at the wreck before the gentry or the Receiver of Wrecks did. Foremost on the scene would be the miners. Mine managers and shareholders -they were known as captains and adventurers - bitterly complained that a wreck in the vicinity meant no work in the mine that day. The word would go round, as swiftly a thousand feet underground as to the labourer at the plough. Then the miners would swarm to surface up their crazy, interminable lengths of wooden ladder to erupt with axe or pick on their shoulders, and the candle stuck with clay on their felt hats still smoking, and rampage to the shore.

On this occasion - it was 20th March 1817 - the Ilfracombe brig 'Mary' went aground in a blizzard at eight bells in the dark of the middle watch on Fassel Geaver sands. Fassel Geaver is a cove close by Hell's Mouth, that aptly named overhang you reach soon after passing the site of the 'dig', and where you gaze giddily down to the surf a two hundred foot pebble drop straight below. Access to the little cove is by a cliff path, up which Captain Bowden, leaving a duty watch aboard, climbed with his crew after mooring his ship until tide and weather should let them get her off. For the 'Mary' was none the worse for grounding. The weary sailors tramped across the headland to Gwithian. The villagers made them welcome and there they stayed, but for relieving the men on guard, honoured guests with even a change of clothes washed by the housewives and hung out to dry.

But they stayed too long. On the second evening the watch turned up before their time with a sorry tale. A mob of tinners had come roaring along the North cliffs from Camborne and down the path to the cove. They cut the brig's cables so that, the tide being out, she keeled over onto the sand. Then they stampeded over the bulwarks, brandishing their axes like the pirates they were, and forced the watchmen to flee for their lives.

The wreckers did not finish their business until they had visited the village and stolen the seamen's clothes from the clothes lines. This vindictive act was perhaps due to the 'Mary's' cargo being culm, a fine coal on its way to the furnaces at Hayle, and as little use in a kitchen range as the black sand of Tahiti and Tenerife it so much resembles. Be that as it may, those Camborne miners were not prepared to allow a shipwrecked stranger even the clothes in his kit bag. Enough that first the sea, and next themselves, had granted him his life! They seized the brig's two anchors and the barrels of beef and biscuits in the hold, took all her cordage, and hacking away such of her spars and timbers as they could get up the cliff left the brig 'Mary,' that had stood so trim to resume her voyage, a wreck.

This time, though, the Camborne tinners did not get away with their infamy. A Camborne magistrate ordered the arrest of the ringleaders, who were carted off to Bodmin gaol for judgement.

As we saw at Bedruthan Steps, although the tin miners were the most expert wreckers, there were many other dwellers on the Cornish coast, and a fair way inland for that matter, who would readily plunder a ship ashore whether she could be salvaged or not. Women wreckers greatly outnumbered the men on Hayle sands one April morning in 1826, where a fine French ship, the 'Ocean', waiting in St. Ives Bay for a fair wind, had parted her cables and driven ashore. The local population for miles around flocked down to the beach and swarmed aboard, the few officers of the law being powerless to stop them. While the men knocked off the heads of casks of wine and scoffed it out of their hats the women, reported the West Briton, "carried off whatever they could lay their hands on, and were very dexterous in concealing bottles of wine and other things, so as to avoid a search." And where would they have concealed their booty but under those voluminous petticoats women wore in past times; and what customs official would dare lift a woman's skirt, however certain he might be that no female who waddled as she did could be carrying aught but contraband? By evening the assembly on the sands had become a drunken orgy, and fun and games, "some of them of the most ludicrous description," took place.

For bulkier items men came into their own. Strandings on Hayle bar are common, and a Hayle resident, seen struggling nearer our own days to carry off a chest from a wreck, was offered a helping hand. No, he could manage all right. "'Tedn' nothin' but sand in 'un." Soon afterwards the wrecker bought a strip of land above the harbour and started Clifton Terrace. Or so I have been told!

Behind this terrace rise the towans, and as you follow the ridge across Riviere you come to Phillack church. Close by is a pub so ancient that even the landlord has not traced its origins. As with all old inns it once brewed its own ale, a popular draught prepared from the well in the yard, the water having a brownish tinge and a distinctive taste which gave body to the brew. Literally so, one day; for the bucket came up containing not so much water as blood. A stabbed corpse was found in the bottom of the well, but who it was no one could say, nor at whose hands the hapless stranger had met his doom. Thereafter the pub, which had been know as the Top of the Nob, was called the Bucket of Blood, but renamed the New Inn in deference to the nicer feelings of a more sophisticated age. Latterly - such are we today! - it is back to the Bucket.

As you would expect, ghostly footsteps and weird noises have been heard there, but no apparitions; though the barman did think he saw someone in the bar long after 'chucking out' time. But old houses talk to themselves, and are a powerful aid to imagination. However, there is good evidence that the Bucket of Blood dispensed a stronger liquor than its own brew, while the delivery of smuggled kegs was as usual obscured by stories of phantoms and unworldly vengeance calculated to keep Phillack heads under the bedclothes on moonshine nights.

One night a year or two ago a young man stepped out alone into the inn yard and the ice-blue suffusion of a Spring full moon. Nearby rooftops and the church tower glimmered in the pallid light; a breeze which surely stole from the graves mounting to the ridge behind the church, out of sight but chillingly in mind, rustled in a tree above his head. And as the young man stood there, nerving himself to brave the creeping fingers of the night of his way home, a voice spoke in the wind. "Hullo! Hullo!" He could not move. But it must be that one pint too many; never another drop should pass his lips. All the old yarns about the hauntings of the Bucket of Blood became present, and real. "Hullo!" He looked up, and saw......

But here a glimpse into the town is called for, down where the St. Erth road winds out of Hayle. 'Bird Paradise' there is a small zoo, mainly for exotic birds. Some are caged, but many fly free, gorgeous parrots and such, returning to their roosts at nightfall as birds do - unless they linger too long and must spend the night away from home. Up in a tree. Up in a tree that shed its leafy shadow on the moon-drenched inn yard of the Bucket of Blood. "Hullo!" A greeting from one belated wanderer to another. The young man looked up, saw the parrot, forswore the pledge, and went back into the pub.

Close by the church and graveyard where our friend had so nearly committed himself to total abstinence, a holy well lost its mystical powers over two centuries and a half ago. This well had been imparting its virtues throughout the parish of Phillack ever since St. Piala evaded King Teudar's clutches, and must have been considered a certainty to continue with the blessed work for as long again. Indeed, under other than Christian auspices it had probably worked its wonders in a subsequent millenium of sun and earth worship. Nevertheless only the village pump, or at any rate the stream that fed it and for that matter supplied the Bucket of Blood with the fundamental of its 'real ale', saw what remained of Phillack Holy Well into the twentieth century. Its sacred properties had been dissipated as told in 1928 by Myrgh Piala, first woman Bard of Cornwall, who was more commonly known as Mrs. Annie Pool.

Hayle Town was yet to be. Phillack Churchtown was all the town there was in the wide-spread parish, Angarrack, Ventonleague and a cluster or two of cottages hidden among trees on the opposite hillside scarcely classifying even as villages. Where Hayle was destined to grow so fast, so soon, there were three manor houses of considerable antiquity, Trevassack at the upper end of the creek, Bodriggy in the middle, and Penpol at its mouth. Each stood in its own estate, with its outhouses, gardens and fields around it, there on the southern side of the long arm of the estuary, its owner fulfilling the busy, if privileged, agrarian duties of a landowner.

Trevassack, described by the scientist-historian Davies Gilbert as "the place of most importance in Phillack", has passed into several hands since the middle ages, until now you can see the house in the extremity of decay, unoccupied, collapsing, yet not quite a ruin. It was Erasmus Pascoe of Trevassack who committed in 1723 that act of sacrilege which robbed the holy well of its sanctity, and bitterly he paid for it. He washed his mangy dog in the well, whether from arrogant disregard of its holiness, or from the hope that even a faithful hound might be cured therein. What happened to the dog is not recorded; Pascoe, though, "died a dreadful

Bucket of Blood Inn, Phillack. Murder most foul.

death" shortly afterwards, his son and heir following him to the grave that same year, his children meeting an untimely end in poverty, and the property "being wasted." As for the well, once profaned its sacred attributes disappeared, and before long it too was gone.

CHAPTER SIX

THE TALE OF A TOWN

Two Cornish villages, Angarrack and St. Erth, met late in life to conceive, so to speak, the town of Hayle. Hayle lies within the parish of Phillack, which centred on Phillack Churchtown, the quiet community on the Towans above the Pool - quiet today, though a hundred years ago the dunes from Riviere to Gwithian smoked and thundered with the mining of silver, lead, copper, tin, arsenic and zinc. And wherever a tin stream swirled rustily down to the sea, teams of 'streamers' desperately splashed and shovelled to win from the 'tailings' tin that had escaped from the mines above. However, Hayle Town had already spread its wings before prospectors delved through the Towans to the rich rock beneath, and in time the activities there ceased and the Churchtown relaxed once more in the peace of the centuries, with little excitement more than parish celebrations at 'Banky Daker' near the site of Teudar's castle on Riviere Towans.

Hayle, until well into the eighteenth century, was no more than its name implies - the river emptying into St. Ives Bay. What buildings there were, apart from three or four manor houses reposing within their estates, were clustered at Lelant and Tredreath, now Lower Lelant, across the water. The West Cornwall highway, not the route you hurtle along nowadays, then dipped into Angarrack, steeply down to the valley and as steeply up the other side, with all the time it took to fix skids on cart wheels for a cautious 1 in 6 descent, to urge exhausted horses up the opposite hill, and then make good the journey to a likely further delay at St. Erth's narrow pack-bridge before at last clattering over the cobbles at Penzance. Today the railway runs parallel to a few sculptured milestones which still flank the old road, while pretty Angarrack village drowses beneath a quite magnificent Victorian viaduct, and cars dodging the holiday traffic cross a bridge documented six years before the battle of Crecy.

Eighteenth century maps show a route, which must be presumed little better than a track, leading from Ventonleague at the innermost end of Phillack creek to Camborne. It was joined there by a similar track from Angarrack, this being largely a link road between Trungle and Angarrack mills and the great mill at Loggans which now derelict and disintegrating and an affront to local environmentalists, commands the eastern approach to Hayle. These three mills once ground the flour for much of West Cornwall. The principal millers were the Hosken family, who in later parnership with Trevithick and Polkinghorne dominated milling from the Truro wharves westward. You would see the letters HTP everywhere, right up to recent years. They would even appear on the Monday clothes lines in the lesser farmyards, linen flour bags retaining the indelible black monogram though fashioned into shirts and shifts and more intimate 'free traders'. still remembered as such, but why so called yet another mystery of yesterday's Cornwall.

The Angarrack river is a tributary of the Hayle, and the town started to grow at their confluence, where it flowed into Phillack creek now enclosed as a principal factor in the development of the town. The village lay within the enormous, Saxon-established manor of Conerton, never part of the Duchy of Cornwall, but Earl Arundel of Wardour land from 1100 until the break-up of the Arundel estates in 1803. Except for its two flour mills Angarrack was a wholly farming community, till the industrial revolution came to West Cornwall. It came early. It began in 1692 with a stamping mill at Hillside, Angarrack. A generation later the London firm Francis Moult and Sons opened next door the smelting house which today bears the legend 1706, and has been caringly incorporated into the village garage. Tin was smelted there, the more difficult and costly process for copper not yet having found a foothold in Cornwall. But when in 1808 mining began to ravish the lush countryside of the valley village, it was a rich lode of copper ore that was shovelled into sacks and panniers and hauled across the marshes to the Copperhouse furnaces for smelting. At the height of the Napoleonic wars, with copper in demand for sheathing the bottoms of the world-wide wooden navy against the depredations of the teredo worm, and with copper and tin needed for the bronze cannons of both services, the village played its full part in the metal output of Cornwall. And that tin too was the chief ingredient then of common tableware you could have seen at the Angarrack Inn, opened two years before the discovery of copper at its doorstep. Its row of pewter tankards catered for smelters and miners and teamsters, even ship builders for a while, and then of bridge builders and masons and their back-up gangs, for eighty prosperous years, with as many more of tranquil oblivion until the charm of a pretty village, with Everyman and his car, crowded the bar again.

Back in the mid-1700's a Camborne company, opposed though it was by powerful Welsh and Bristol smelters, had developed the techniques of copper smelting. As the Cornish Copper Company and with a formidable array of big-wig directors, it moved in 1758 to Ventonleague where grazing land rolled down to Phillack creek. Here the Angarrack and other local ores were smelted, though after 1819 shipped once again to the Severn, it proving more rewarding to import Welsh coal for the mines rather than use it up in the Company furnaces. Neighbouring Wheal (mine) Alfred, most of its fifteen hundred miners settling on Copper Company land, achieved spectacular success, and as spectacularly failed, even though its galleries ran, like roots seeking water, under Angarrack and half way to Troon. But when after years of steady production the

Angarrack lodes, too, were worked out, the tin smelter still roared and belched until the '80's. Then, with the replacement (1882-5) of the first railway viaduct to span the valley, Angarrack relapsed again into Arcadian seclusion.

ANGARRACK

Under its viaduct the village doses.
Though rush of wheels - and world - reverberates,
Remote in tip-toe hush of fruit and roses
Itself alone Angarrack contemplates.

Trains doppler-rumble overhead to Hayle;
So runs the world, strident, impermanent!
The viaduct abides, spans the still vale,
Tops roofs, trees, gardens, weed-dark stream, content.

No smooth content a century before!
Stonemasons hammer, 'midst the busy din
Chisel the granite; blocks squeal, scaffolds soar;
Pier beyond pier, arch beside arch, begin

To rival the proud aqueducts of Rome.
Sun drops to chimneys, supper smoke ascends,
Loosed horses trot to grass, miners trudge home,
Blasting thuds underground, the full day ends.

Folk whose ox-wains had crossed, since Crecy year,
At Mellenvrane this pack-bridge to the mill
Sank mines, built chapel and inn; Wesley preached here,
Watt engines chain-hauled trucks up Steamers Hill.

Now such as I, Time's memory-banks, stay talking,
Trim lawns, watch telly, snooze, await school bus,
Mums with prams, workers, shoppers driving, walking,
Homing through honeysuckle lanes to us.

But developers and planners in collusion
Shop-floors would on your quiet fields construct,
Though lovely your lewth, Angarrack, rare seclusion
Lotus-houred beneath your viaduct.

Hayle Town came into the world under the name of Copperhouse. The Copper House (1784), now no more, had been a round chapel. Though

Angarrack, at the village pump. Courtesy David Clarke. "Under its viaduct the village dozes."

you may picture it as gleaming red-gold, a sort of colossal copper kettle, and John Wesley liked it, it would instead have been a meeting house of sepulchral aspect. This was because the slag from the smelter had been cast in blocks (the concrete version being a hundred and fifty years off conception) black and hard as iron and still everywhere around. They were used for building copper men's cottages, the chapel, walls much further afield, and later on the 'Black Road' and its bridge that you see spanning the head of the Pool to the company quay.

Hayle, with its phenomenal mining and foundry development, depended on the sea to carry fuel to its industries and cargoes to its customers. The first port of the Hayle River was naturally sited where the river reacted to the tide and widened to an estuary. This was at St. Erth, which despite the ravages of the sand contrived somehow to stay in business until the first quarter of the last century. One of the invading saints, Irishman Erc, Bishop of Slane in County Meath, had followed the east bank of the estuary and settled where his name was to be perpetuated, albeit long after his death in 514. For according to the geographer-prehistorian Ivor Thomas, who researched the 'Isthmus of Penwith' soon after the war, the ancient Cornish knew the church there as Lanhudnow, the monastery of Udnow, whoever he may have been. Formerly on a hill above the river where an earthwork can be traced, it moved down to the Hayle as trading facilities grew, monks being then, as now, concerned with building and trade besides the spiritual demands of their calling. Domesday Book makes no mention of St. Erth, but refers to Trewinnard, where the manor house, after centuries of changing fortunes and rebuilding in the 1700's, is now the home of Sir John Nott, latest and most eminent of several MP's to live there. However, the port at the head of the estuary was certainly St. Erth when the pack bridge was constructed there around 1300, so Erc came into his own at last. Apart from the bridge at St. Erth, and the immemorial ferry at the seaward end of the estuary, the only way to cross the river was a hazardous journey over the sands at the ebb, until the causeway built in 1825 hastened you into the Penwith peninsula and stopped up St. Erth for good.

But from the days when the Irish curachs had paid toll to King Teudar, and goodness knows how long before, ships had sailed up to St. Erth from "the broad-bosomed ocean." Cargoes were there transferred to pack animals, which alone could travel the tracks that passed for roads three centuries back, and which followed the age-old route to Ictis, later the Pilgrims' Way when St. Michael's Mount became as famous a sanctuary as its mother-monastery in France. Crosses and forts, or what little is left of them, mark the Pilgrims' Way. At some stage in the four-mile journey across the isthmus the bridle path widened sufficiently to become a cart track, for early reports mention waggons arriving at the Mount.

Although as with so much of the north coast of Cornwall the

Hayle 1895. Courtesy David Clarke.

estuary had been silting up, in the late eighteenth century ships still, when the tide must have been very high and the river bed beneath the arches dredged to bed-rock, got beyond St. Erth bridge to where the Battery Mills with their five water-wheels provided a copper sheathing service for ships bottoms. Battery Stamping Mills were owned by the Cornish Copper Company, and in 1784 Mr. Gilbert of Phillack was its manager. Today all that remains of its considerable properties is a mushroom farm.

But the sand, which Hayle learnt to control but has never beaten, was not to be denied. Deep-sea vessels could get up to St. Erth only in special circumstances, and at last not at all. Wharves had to be provided downstream at Tredreath, now Lower Lelant. For Lelant Churchtown, seaport in the age of the Plantagenets, had vanished under the sand. Griggs Quay, at the St. Ives end of the causeway, came into being where formerly a heath plant of that name had blanketed the water-front. There were also wharves at Hayle-to-be.

First of the Hayle wharves was constructed by Lemon and Company, but the man on the spot was John Curnow, a self-made man honoured in the annals of Hayle Town as 'Merchant' Curnow. He was managing director of the Lemon wharves at Carnsew, and in due course bought up all the local shares. William Lemon's name is great in the story of Cornish mining. The son of a Mounts Bay labourer, he made an immense fortune in the industry and won universal respect. He remarkably educated himself in middle age, at the height of his business ventures, to the extent of reading the classics in their original Greek and Latin. Lemon Street in Truro is named after him. He died, a baronet, in 1760. So many Cornishmen achieved greatness from the humblest origins, in days when pride of birth counted for so much; Passmore Edwards, Opie the painter, Sir Humphry Davy and others. Many famous personages are associated with the developing town of Hayle, from Sir William Lemon to Elizabeth Arden, the cosmetics queen.

Carnsew, where the ancient fort was so strategically sited, was one of two starting places for those who preferred crossing the sands to making a detour over St. Erth bridge. As at the other favoured route - the Royal Standard Inn (once Millwood's or 'The Passage House') to close by Norwayman's Dock at Lelant - posts marked the way across. Given an ebb tide and dry sands it was a reasonably safe crossing for pedestrians and horsemen, but chancey and even downright dangerous for anything much heavier than a donkey-shay, as John Wesley found when he made the trip in a coach in haste to reach St. Ives via Lelant. The Carnsew passage incidentally finished up at Grigg's Quay, for the deep water which in Roman times had allowed ships to approach at any tide belonged to the remote past. These sands played, as you will see, a significant part in promoting that ingenuity which in 1800 gave Hayle comparability to Manchester and superiority to Birmingham, and which established the Copper Company as an enterprise of national - even international - repute.

It was at Carnsew that a foundry took root which challenged the Copper Company. In that challenge were the birth pangs of the new town. The Copper Company was in full fling, its black block township astir with purpose, when a blacksmith named John Harvey moved down from his forge at Gwinear to Carnsew. The year was 1779, he was forty-nine. This move had been prompted by a gentleman who had lost a silver buckle from his shoe, and wanting a quick replacement called at the smithy. "Give me one o' your silver spoons and I'll make you a buckle out of it," said the smith. The speedy result, and the contact thus established, so pleased the gentleman that he urged Harvey to turn his skills to a more rewarding enterprise than a backwoods forge. It is believed that John Harvey's adviser was Sir John St. Aubyn of Clowance, whose descendants' home is now St. Michael's Mount.

Certainly it was on St. Aubyn land that Harvey opened up at Carnsew. But not as a blacksmith. As a side line he had previously made wooden pipes for the new-fangled steam pumps which enabled lodes to be worked at lower levels than before, Cornish mines being subject to flooding at sea level. Some were already running under the sea bed. As deeper galleries branched ever further from the main shafts, he foresaw a growing demand for iron piping for the pumps, to which end he traded scrap metal for the ready-made article. By 1790 Harvey had cemented a business connection with Abraham Darby's famous iron foundry at Coalbrookdale in the Severn valley, the pipes being delivered to Bristol, whence he shipped them to his Carnsew wharf at Hayle.

The next move was to master the craft of casting his own pipes. To do this it is said that, concealing his status as master smith, he took a job as a journeyman at a South Wales foundry and learnt the business thoroughly. Soon John Harvey was not only producing at his own foundry the pump pipes for the Cornish mines, he was making the pumps too, shipping the raw material from his Coalbrookdale associates and the culm, the fine coal for his furnaces, from their Welsh subsidiaries. At John Harvey's death in 1803 his foundry was already big business.

Far bigger business was the Cornish Copper Company, which was lavishing funds on the town it was deliberately bringing to life. With practical men such as Sampson Swaine on its board, and rich and illustrious 'adventurers' or shareholders who represented much of the parliamentary and landed interests of West Cornwall, it had come far since that first smelter at Ventonleague. The moving spirit of the company was John Edwards of Ludgvan, a man every way as considerable as old John Harvey and John's only surviving son and successor Henry - a man who would never admit defeat and was jealous, moreover, of his rights as first in the field. The prosperity of both Foundry - as the Harvey end of the emerging town came to be known - and Copperhouse depended on shipping, and shipping was the vexed question which was to lead to blows.

Ten years before John Harvey forsook Gwinear to take on the 'establishment', the Copper Company had completed the formidable undertaking of digging a half-mile canal alongside the shallow creek to bring deep sea vessels right up to the works, with floodgates and sluices at the wharf to keep the canal clear of sand. It all looks to this day like a backwater at Amsterdam; and in fact Hayle has links with the Zuider Zee which were yet to be forged.

These experiments in water engineering proving successful, John Edwards' next move was to dispel the sand that was choking the estuary, the channel of the conjoined Hayle, Angarrack and Penpol rivers constantly changing course and a bar building up across the mouth of the estuary: which is how you see it at present, now that the harbour is no longer sluiced, while only small boats put to sea from what in the last century was a port of registry, and the one north coast harbour of refuge west of Padstow. The company mastered the obstructing sand with consummate skill, damming Phillack creek so that it became today's placid pool, swans and all (a post-war bonus). Flood-gates operated to retain the water at high tide, and release it an hour before full ebb, in a torrent that scoured the channel. By 1808 two more flood-gates had been installed and large coasters of up to 120 tons tied up at Copperhouse quay, while within the next thirty years the Foundry Company's pool at Carnsew was also gushing over the sands. If ever the harbour is to admit deep sea vessels again, and its wharves to bustle with the marine activities which up to a few years ago were so necessary a part of the life of Hayle, those sluices will have to gush again. It is sad to see the decay of a once busy and notable port. Well, you never know!

By 1819 the Cornish Copper Company had shut down its smelting works, shipping the ore as formerly to Swansea, where the process was more economically completed near the coal mines. The closure of the plant cost many men their livelihood, until they were absorbed into the Copperhouse foundry which became a further challenge to Harvey's next year. The finish of the smelter had its compensations. Fumes of arsenic were emitted during smelting, bringing to an early grave as many victims as the dreaded miners' disease, and producing a Copperhouse populace pathetically at odds with the apple-cheeked seamen who brought the ships up-canal. Iron for the foundry and coal for its furnaces, and the mines that were its customers, were now unloaded at Copperhouse and the ore shipped there for the return voyage.

Long before the Copper Company and Harvey's foundries were in competition, John Edwards and John Harvey were at loggerheads, a confrontation which lasted until not so long ago when Copperhouse and Foundry boys fought 'tob' (turf) battles, and the representatives on the old Hayle Urban District Council were so perpetually at odds that Hayle lost its U.D.C. and was merged into the now defunct West Penwith Council.

Copper Company vessels shipped Harvey's coal and pig iron from the Bristol Channel at monopoly charges. These persuaded Harvey to provide his own transport. In 1787 he purchased the sloop 'Providence', first of the Harvey fleet. Edwards took this as posing a threat to his company's all-important coal trade with the local mines. Accordingly he bought out Messrs. Harris and Ellis, mine factors, whose property lay north of Harvey's at Merchant Curnow's quay. Squire Harris's land at Rosewarne now includes the experimental horticultural station. Vestiges of Thomas Ellis's house survive beneath the viaduct at Foundry. His descendant, Major Tom Ellis, lives at the ancient Arundell manor house, Penpol, nearby. This take-over left Harvey's with no access to the sea except up the Penpol River at high tide. Permission having been granted by Earl Arundell of Wardour, landlord of most of Phillack parish in 1793, the foundrymen were then put to work deepening the little river. The Coppermen filled it up again. Litigation became the order of the day. Hayle's split personality, or its corporate equivalent, is only now healing over.

At this stage the conflict was all about the mine supply business, both companies investing in the mines which were burrowing ever wider and deeper beneath West Cornwall, and expecting a fair trade return therefrom. The Cornish Company accordingly resorted to violence, launching a campaign of harassment in 1795. They would force Harvey's to confine their activities to the foundry, where East and West Hayle were not yet rivals. Copper men filled in a leat which drove Harvey's boring mill, almost bringing the water wheel to a halt. They boarded a Harvey ship just home from Plymouth with a cargo of limestone, and tipping it onto the sand carted much of it away to their own kilns. Claiming as theirs a plot at Carnsew on which Harvey's had stacked their timber, brought at great cost to Norwayman's Dock below Lelant church by large Scandinavian full-riggers, and transferred to lighters for the short trip up-river, they threw it into the tide with pumps and castings there. Then forty or so more Copperhouse invaders dismantled a lighter being built on Foundry stocks and practically wrecked it. All this was justified on the grounds of trespass. But the Foundry Company persevered.

Harvey's involvement with wealthy 'adventurers' such as the Copper Company attracted was not an unqualified success. Family marriages compensated. John's eldest daughter married the mechanic William West, his capable and ever loyal lieutenant. Jane's husband was the brilliant if erratic inventor Richard Trevithick, whose steam locomotive - the first practical 'loco' in the world - took to the road at Camborne in 1801. Some ascribe to this epoch-making trial the ditty "Going up Camborne hill coming down" that you hear more often in West Cornwall than 'Trelawny.' Eventually Richard deserted wife, home and the company for silver mining in Peru. He became a 'freedom fighter' there, ultimately returning to England 'broke.' Unsuccessfully petitioning parliament for financial help on account of his inventions, he died at Dartford in 1833, in abject poverty. Like Sir Goldsworthy Gurney a luckless man! But there was the aura of greatness about him.

As for the neglected Jane, Harvey's installed her as manager of an inn they built to employ her housekeeping talents in the entertainment of clients from afar. Named the 'White Hart', it is today the Masonic Hall. The present large hotel conjoined to it and bearing its name dates from 1838. It stood across Foundry Square opposite one of the earliest railway stations ever, erected as the terminus of the Hayle Railway in 1837. It was only recently demolished, before the replacement by dull and often dirty diesels of gleaming, lovingly tendered engines redolent of oily steam - a loving care that has produced the Railway Buff, dedicated to the preservation of rail antiquities. 'Buffs' will have to stay alert if other relics of the old line are to survive. The new A30 has bull-dozed a stretch of it.

The death of John Harvey in 1803 left the Foundry Company short of his skills as a master craftsman. In his father's stead Henry Harvey, with an eye for a good man, engaged a West Cornwall engineer called Arthur Woolf as Company Superintendent. Trevithick had pioneered Harvey's famous Cornish boiler. It was Woolf who constructed a wrought iron version able to withstand the increasing pressures of the new age of steam. As a practical engineer, if not an inventor, Woolf had little to learn from his contemporary Richard Trevithick.

1816, and peace in the air! Centuries of French wars were at an end and Napoleon was safely out of the way at last. Even Harvey's and the Copper Company declared a truce. Copper ore required special handling. Ore in excess of what the still active smelter could consume was sorted and heaped on mats woven from the marram grass that binds Riviere towans, of which the Copper Company claimed ownership. Then off it went to the Swansea smelters in the vessels that had brought the company coal, an in-out traffic with a pay-off both ways. But Harvey's had no wharves adequate for sorting and piling copper ore awaiting transport; their ships had to return empty. Henry Harvey and Joseph Carne, Copper Company manager since John Edwards' death in 1807, accordingly signed an agreement to their mutual benefit. Foundry ships were to have access, at a price, to Copper Company's quays, on condition that only Harvey's own vessels, at the time a sloop and a couple of brigantines, were employed. The old Copperhouse dread of competition in the coal trade to the mines was still paramount. However Harvey's captains were soon complaining that their ships were being denied their proper turn at the quays, so Henry Harvey again focussed his attention on the Penpol River.

The Copper Company had allowed their Carnsew quay to silt up. You will recall that they had acquired it from Messrs. Harris and Ellis only to forestall Harvey's breaking out into the harbour they regarded as their

Richard Trevithick
The inventor with model of his first practical steam locomotive.

Courtesy David Clarke.

Foundry Square, Hayle, c. 1845. The railway station, built 1837, was opposite the White Hart Hotel and beneath where the viaduct now spans the U-bend at Foundry. Courtesy Royal Institute of Cornwall.

own, and they hung on to that spit of land near the foundry like a dog in a manger. Now on the death of the third life on which the Copper Company's leasehold was based (a system prevalent in Cornwall years ago) most of the Carnsew estate passed to a new clutch of owners. These included the two progressive Members of Parliament James Halse of St. Ives and Squire Praed of Lelant, who allowed Harvey's the lease in the teeth, you may well imagine, of Joseph Carne. Henry Harvey then set about straightening and deepening the Penpol river, to build that long quay there which juts well out into the harbour. You see it across the river just before you reach the viaduct at Foundry. Fishing boats moor there now, where Harvey ships made fast, thrusting their bowsprits across the slightly angled dockside, and where later on mounds of scrap metal overshadowed some once splendid hull disintegrating on the mud.

The work on the river bed involved much digging out of mud and sand. One May morning in 1818 Henry Harvey's scouts informed him that Copperhouse was on the move, and no sooner had he reinforced his workmen there than the invaders marched in. Each man on either side flourished a shovel - a Cornish shovel like a curved quarter-staff with a great wide spearhead set aslant. The wonder is that the sands did not run red as when King Teudar greeted the saints thirteen hundred years before. In fact no one was injured, though all day long the mud and sand was shovelled out by Foundry, and back by Copperhouse, until the evening tide forced a draw. Through the night Henry hired labourers and carts from far and wide, and next day the river bed was loaded into the carts and driven away, to the confusion of the Copper men. Henry Harvey and Joseph Carne then signed an agreement. Each was to construct a quay either side of the Penpol river, the Copper Company's that at the ninety degree turn in the road where Millwood's House, now the Royal Standard Inn, fortified its customers for the hazardous crossing of the sands to Norwayman's Dock at Lelant. This was on part of the Carnsew estate owned by the St. Aubyns.

It was Harvey's turn as Cock o' the Walk. The course of the Penpol river had always marked the boundary between Phillack and St. Erth parishes. Though it had been changed by the work on the channel, Henry erected stone markers which not only outlined the ancient boundary but claimed land for Harvey's that Joseph Carne insisted was his. Actions for trespass and such coming to nought, the Copper Company again resorted to force. On Sunday night, 16th November, when all good church and chapel folk should have been quietly at home, a cluster of lantern lights was seen on a spit of sand at the river mouth which had built up on the diversion of the current, and on which Harvey's had placed the demarcation stones. Forty or so Copper men were rolling the stones into the river. A like number of Foundry men drove them off, but next morning the struggle was resumed with hundreds engaged on either side, the Copper Company now planting their own markers on the sand-spit while Harvey's heaved them away. Henry was knocked down, and there the contestants stood, threatening and shouting and thwacking at each other with bloodshed imminent. Eventually a magistrate, the vicar of St. Erth, sent for by Henry Harvey who was his most munificent parishioner, arrived with the full paraphernalia of his office to read the Riot Act. Then he required the principals to meet him at Millwood's and sign a treaty of non-aggression. Soon afterwards the Copper Company went out of smelting and into the foundry business.

Whatever the consequences for the new town - and you may regret that the Cornish Copper Company did not survive, to maintain the lock gates, clear the waterways, and develop the wharves and warehouses that the Foundry Company let decay before gasping out its last breath in the uncaring arms of up-country financiers - competition between the opposite ends of Hayle achieved extraordinary results. You would scarcely credit that Copperhouse boilers and mining machinery were in world-wide demand from Moscow to Montevideo. That the Copper Company, soon to be known as Sandys, Carne and Vivian, built the 'Cornubia' locomotive for the Hayle Railway only nine years after George Stephenson's 'Rocket' hit contemporary headlines (with all its unacknowledged obligations to Cornish inventors). That it supplied the major parts of engines which transformed offshore Holland into farmland. That it forged the links of Clifton Suspension Bridge and many of those which bear you safely more than a century later as your train crosses the Tamar over Brunel's historic bridge. Bells of tin and copper alloy that chime you to prayer at St. Ives, Helston and other parish churches in West Cornwall were cast at Copperhouse. Nor were the company's services to shipping confined to docks and marine engines. Few now recall that the Company built fine iron-hulled sailing vessels, the last in 1866. After that Pool's of Copperhouse, today Hayle's chief employer of labour, built a few ships too.

But it was Harvey's who won international recognition as shipbuilders. Between 1834 and '93 wooden sloops, brigs and brigantines, schooners and luggers were the first to slide down the slipway into the great pool they had enclosed at Carnsew, principally to scour their channels as the Copper Company did theirs from the Phillack pool. Then paddle-wheelers and later screw steamers took to the tide. Iron ships followed iron-framed wooden ships, and steel freighters reached their acme in SS. 'Ramleh' of 3,800 tons, for size and power surpassing most of its contemporaries. But by the time of the great Queen's Golden Jubilee ships were no longer built at Hayle and the slow, sad decline of the foundry began. When old shipwright Henry Warren had been retired complaining, he prophesied that he would live to see the grass grow over the Carnsew yard. He did! Even ship-breaking, which survived off and on eighty years more, came to an end in the 1970's. And now the whole harbour has surrendered to the long sleep of the sands.

Impressive as were the achievements of both rival foundries, the comparison is best illustrated by the two Cornish engines, built for the London Water Board and still intact, though unused these many years, in the old waterworks at Kew. The older engine was made by Sandys, Carne and Vivian in 1846. It has a magnificent 90-inch cylinder. The other, from Harvey's foundry twenty-five years later, has an even more magnificent cylinder, a hundred inches in diameter. Foundry had the edge on Copperhouse all along the line, perhaps because its affairs were largely in the hands of craftsmen who valued professional pride as highly as profit. John Harvey was a blacksmith, John Edwards "had been recommended at a very early age to some situation requiring talent." Henry Harvey had been brought up in the foundry business. Joseph Carne was a banker's son. And so on.

Perhaps, though, Harvey's Foundry out-did and out-lived the Copperhouse Foundry through operating right on the estuary instead of at the upper end of a creek, alternative avenues of transport - the causeway and the turnpike road (1825 and '40) that is now the A30, and the developing railway system - hardly favouring one more than the other. And perhaps sheer hatred and the "Anything you can do I can do better" syndrome drove Harvey's to excel, competition deciding the issue.

These competing masterpieces emerged from a little town which did not even know its own name until the rival nominations of Copperhouse and Carnsew were dismissed in favour of the river that was its life. The 'West Briton' had reported in April 1825 "the intention of the inhabitants of Copperhouse in the harbour of Hayle to.... discard the present name of their popular and overgrown village, and to substitute a more appropriate one; Mining Port has been suggested." Well, a public meeting was convened shortly after and the name Hayle chosen. Copperhouse, you observe, was still the dominant end of the town.

But what took shape, or was predestined, in the huddle of workshops at Carnsew, and then in the Foundry complex - in that majestic granite building you pass on turning onto the Helston road and could mistake for a relic of some Golden Age - which made so disproportionate an impact on the age of steam? The sections of Richard Trevithick's 'fire carriage', which you have already pictured trundling up Camborne hill and into history with a song, were made there though assembled at Camborne. Three of his Cornish boilers won a government contract for the Royal Mail Steam Packet 'Echo', and led the company into big-time shipbuilding. Harvey's Cornish Engine found a market wherever in the world there was that hole, as was said, at the bottom of which a Cornishman hacked away at the living rock. And so, to be fair, did the Copperhouse model.

The giant pumps, Harvey's the larger, proudly preserved at the old

Kew waterworks were surpassed when Nicholas Harvey contracted with the Dutch for draining the Zuider Zee, a major role shared with Copperhouse and Fox of Falmouth's Perran Foundry. Harvey's supplied cylinders and engine parts together with the complete Cornish engine, one of their cylinders measuring a whole 12 feet in interior diameter and rocking eleven great pumping beams. You could drive a waggon and horses through it. This monster was shipped for Texel in June 1844 in the Harvey-built and owned ketch 'Carnsew.' She was an 80-tonner lengthened, strengthened and rerigged for the job, but still her hold was little wider than the boiler. Captain Clarke found his ship leaky, his compass faulty, and reported "a troublesome passage." Small wonder with so tight a fit, so cumbersome a cargo, and so much iron to deflect his compass bearings! But he made it.

An entire engine with a cylinder of the same dimensions was ordered by the Dutch, highly satisfied customers, for draining the Haarlem Meer. It was to be named after Nicholas Samuel Cruquius, a famous pioneer of Lowland reclamation, and it is a tribute to the Cornish company that the engineer in charge of the project was William Husband, an ex-apprentice, with under him John West and a team of Harvey mechanics. Delivered in February 1849, when installed it lifted up 112 tons of water ten feet at a single stroke. The Cruquius was the largest and most powerful steam engine the world had known. It was thundering away eighty-four years later, after which it was retired in honour as a national memorial. A memorial to the reclamation of seventy square miles of top-grade agricultural land, and also to the three giant engines from Cornwall, two of them joint productions of the Foundry, Copperhouse and Perran companies, the third, and greatest, and still maintained for you to see, the Cruquius engine of Harvey's of Hayle.

Henry Harvey's nephew Nicholas Harvey (born of a Helston Harvey, no relative to the Hayle Harveys, and Henry's sister Anne) had contacts with Germany which led to the foundry building a tug for towing a string of Rhine barges. Orders for two similar paddle-wheel tugs were ordered for Holland, the second delivered after Henry's death. Far-seeing industrialists saw the Trevithick boiler as being of revolutionary design and the last word in marine engineering. So revolutionary was it, in fact, that when the R.M.S.P. 'Echo' was doing her trials with a Royal Naval crew the 'black gang' below, hostile to change as they sometimes are even today, did their best to wreck the boilers. But Harvey's beat them.

Both companies manufactured, besides massive engines and ships' ironmongery, all the usual products of a foundry. Oddities from Harvey's indicate an extraordinary range: iron chamber pots at 2½d. (1p) a dozen; 600 tons of perfectly spherical 12, 18 and 20 pounder cannon balls of precise weight and diameter; bronze and iron drawing-room and parlour ornaments known after an earlier Soho line as 'Hayle Toys.' Old John

Harvey had tried his hand at bell founding, casting a 900 lb. tenor for Stithians church near Redruth. Not long ago it was retuned in Leicestershire, and still rings loud and true. But the laurels for the bells go to Copperhouse. At times the two companies did co-operate. In 1836 they united in demanding of the government a custom house for Hayle. It is that lone building between the iron swing-bridge and the town swimming pool. They also jointly sought Hayle's appointment as a Port of Registry, a distinction which endured from 1864 to '82, when the shipping using the harbour, once so numerous, declined.

In the middle of the town's century of triumph - and dissent - the Hayle Steamship Company, with Henry Harvey a considerable shareholder, ran a return passenger and cargo service to Bristol, though only the third paddle-steamer of the line, the 'Cornubia', was built at Foundry. Hayle was no stranger to steamships, one having called in, London-bound from Glasgow, in 1815. The Copper Company constructed the 'Steam Packet' wharf. The Steampacket Inn there, where the easternmost sluice emptied into the estuary, entertained passengers awaiting embarkation. SS 'Cornubia', a graceful, yacht-like beauty, served on the Bristol run for only three years, after which she went to war. During the American civil war the Confederates bought her to run the Union blockade. She was caught and sunk. Shipbuilding at Hayle finished with the closing down of the foundry, which had ceased to pay its way, at the end of the century. What hard times those were for Cornwall! But small naval craft were built at Hayle in the 1939-'45 war. The Hayle Steamship Company failed once you could travel by the Great Western Railway, which absorbed all the minor companies when Brunell's bridge ran it into Cornwall, all the way from Paddington without changing. Today Hayle, pioneer of a sea-rail service to the metropolis, operating a railway only twelve years after the world's first, the Stockton-Darlington line, has had to plead with British Rail for stops at Hayle minimally adequate for the town's growing holiday industry!

Mention of holiday, after so much strife and stress and bursting at the industrial seams, leads to a couple of sports items not to be ignored. Edmund Hockin, son of the Rector of Phillack who bought Riviere towans at the break-up of the Copper Company's land, introduced Rugby football to the Cornish, since when they have been as fanatically rugger minded as their cousins the Welsh. Cricket, where the Cornish are right up top in national inter-village competition, has never attained top county level, not through lack of enthusiasm and ability, but due to the problem of finding and maintaining wide flat outfields. Nevertheless the great ones of cricket used to visit us. Jack Hobbs and Surrey wicket-keeper Herbert Strudwick played in an annual match at Penzance in the '20's. In the early days of the game the famous Lilleywhite visited these parts. Here he was shown a bat, fashioned not as was common out of a single piece of wood, but with a handle of springier wood spliced in. This was the bat made and used by a keen Hayle cricketer called Christophers. It so impressed Lilleywhite that before long spliced bats were in universal use. Miss A.G. Digues La Touche, whose sports stories these are, together with much more about the Hayle of yesteryear, does not say whether Christophers benefited thereby. Mr. Lilleywhite certainly did. An oblique link with the Oxford and Cambridge boat race is provided by the Rev. Hockin. His attachment to a stove-pipe hat green with age was remarked on in the parish. "'Ow don't 'ee get thyself a new 'at, sir?" his flock made bold to ask. "Why should I?" retorted his reverence. "Everyone knows me here." When he was about to go up to London for the boat race, it was assumed that he'd buy himself a new hat for the occasion. "Why should I?" he said. "Nobody knows me there."

It had been a proud day for Harvey's when in 1867 one of their ships, its house flag flying, sailed up the canal to Copperhouse foundry. The mining depression had ruined the Copper Company, and apart from such purchases as Riviere towans Harvey's bought them up, wharves, harbour and all, selling the foundry machinery to the company's old customers in Moscow. Henceforward Hayle practically lived and fed by fiat of the Foundry company, albeit Ellis's Brewery supplied its liquid needs. But the writing was on the wall for Harvey's foundry. It collapsed soon after completing two of its outstanding triumphs. A spring had threatened the Great Western Railway's Severn tunnel project, but six Harvey giants were called to the rescue and the flood water contained and sealed. SS. 'Ramleh', towering above the rooftops from the slipway and a large ship by any standard, had been the pride of Hayle. But at its launching in 1891 up-country competition rendered another such ambitious venture unviable. If only Harvey's and the Copper Company had co-operated instead of being so consistently at loggerheads!

Harvey's continued in business as merchants until a few years ago. In 1902 they negotiated a 99-year lease with the Cornwall Electric Power Company. The generating station, and later an Imperial Chemical Industries factory, brought trade and a steady flow of colliers and coasters to the long north quay and employment to the town. The two enormous buildings, tall chimney stacks and all, loomed ponderously above the wharves and pyramids of Welsh coal in the coal bays. All gone! Sluice gates no longer flush the river beds and 'lagoon' where the wind jammers used to anchor, and sweep the clogging sand into St. Ives Bay, to build up the holiday beaches for miles around. The number of vessels running the sand-bank gauntlet in storm and fog once justified the lifeboat stationed at Hayle just before the demise of the Copper Company. It did stirling work, but post-war depression closed it down in 1920. At present pleasure craft and small fishing boats ply along the estuary and brave the tumbling bar. Nothing more - yet.

A couple of sizeable factories, a growing resort industry, a proliferation of small businesses promise well. The quarrel between East and West Hayle is resolved. There is a will to revive the town, this time on a North-South axis of tourism and trade, acres of derelict land are plums for developers, and the future is heavy with expectancy. Much depends on whether the new trunk road, and the existing railway system, can handle the freight formerly carried by sea. Otherwise the harbour asleep in the sand must awaken and its sluices flow, so that seaborne trade may again come and go. It is still the sand that is the problem; the soft white sand beloved of sunbathers and children; the devouring sand that choked the ports of St. Erth and Lelant and now is digesting the port of Hayle.

There will be those who are concerned that much of interest has been omitted from this Tale of a Town. So, alas, it has! But you can't have it "all to once," as they say hereabouts; not in a chapter or two. Perhaps enough has been told to slow up your urge to penetrate further into Penwith, and to tempt you to look around Hayle Town awhile; and looking around to conjure up, "warts and all", a teeming activity which served an awakening world amid furnace fumes, the spars of fine ships afloat or building, and an eager people touchy with pride in their new town. Then find your way to the beaches. You will long to stay.

Copper Company bells ring you to church all over Cornwall.

6 were chiming at Helston	in 1825
1 at St. Martin-in-Meneage	in 1826
1 at Tintagel	in 1828
2 at Morvah	in 1828
4 at Mullion	in 1828
2 at St. Ives	in 1830
1 at Breage	in 1831
1 at Grade	in 1832
1 at Perranuthnoe	in 1832

Harvey's cast bells for St. Hilary, Illogan, Madron and Stithians. In 1983 a company with the exotic name TEKOA bought up the derelict Harvey empire in Hayle. It is an enterprise viewed with hope by the many, with dismay by some, and as 'pie in the sky' by not a few. But that is tomorrow's story.

CHAPTER SEVEN

RESCUES, RASCALS & A PICNIC

Throughout 'the Season', and particularly when the Clerk of the Weather is in mellow mood, holiday-makers at St. Ives pack piers and quays and adjoining streets. The occasional car, the rest having abandoned the attempt, grumbles along Fore Street or probes the throng outside Hart's ice cream parlour on the wharf and the Sloop Inn next door; but mostly the din of the internal combustion age has yielded to the hubbub of a dozen different tongues and dialects, the shuffle of unhurrying feet, the catcalls of swooping seagulls. It is all remarkably pleasant, at any rate for visitors with time to spare for the leisure life, while 'locals' who sigh for the season's end would sigh the more were it never to begin. Summer beaches teem with sunworshippers, the sea with pleasure boats and surf boards and splashers and swimmers, the more adventurous beguiled for several seasons by 'close encounters' with a friendly dolphin, Beaky, whose return, like King Arthur's, is some day expected.

At such times, though you may perhaps entertain doubts as to a snowy cumulus piling up west of Clodgy or that touch of pink you spotted in the morning sky, 'storm and tempest' are beyond contemplation. It may surprise you to know, therefore, that on estimate forty-three gales (of Force 8 or more) hit the South West every year. Of course, most of them arouse no further comment than a moan or two about the vagaries of British weather. A gust which would rip the tiles off half the roofs in Luton or Leicester glides off the 'broom-shanked' - the cement brushed - slates Down'long with but a sqawk of protest from perching gulls, which with the decline of fishing and the absence of trimmings and offal in the harbour have taken to town life and a sophisticated diet.

But there are occasions, mostly in midwinter, when you would hardly recognise St. Ives, or any other Cornish haven, as your favoured holiday haunt. The harbour heaves, boats toss and jerk at moorings while the waves thunder outside, combers that hump the horizon come rolling into the bay to curve and crash on the beach or explode in leaping fans of foam up and over the cliff. The few who needs must be about in the streets and on the wharf, with everywhere the tang and smell of sand and seaweed and brine, hug chin on chest the shelter of doorways at each frenzy of the gale. But you will always find some stout souls peering seaward, with stinging eyes and the breath half driven back into their lungs, at the terrible, arresting spectacle of primeval forces unleashed. It is an experience for the city dweller to savour, thanking God that when the maroon is fired there are the sea-wise and the brave to man the lifeboat, and launch her into the surf, without asking more of him than his prayers.

Storms burst upon us suddenly. As sudden, sometimes, is the transition from turmoil to calm, when the sun breaks through the cloud-wrack, and the sky clears, and where yesterday the long rollers crashed the wavelets lap around the rocks and purl upon the sand. But the aftermath lingers in banks of weed torn from the sea bed, the debris of wave-swept, often wave-demolished decks and wreckage, always the pitiful remains of sea birds and, once in a while, of such as you and I.

No St. Eian (if Eia, patron saint and name-giver of St. Ives will allow the term!) will ever forget the closing hours of the last day of January, 1938. At 8 p.m. the Panamanian MV. 'Alba', a large freighter of 3,700 tons and with a Hungarian captain and crew, bound for Italy with a cargo of Welsh coal, was caught in the breakers and driven broadside onto Porthmeor beach and the Island rocks. Porthmeor is the surfing beach of seaside St. Ives. For most days of the year a steady swell breaks well out and continues its race to land as an emerald bellied breaker with a mane of spray. But when the storm spirals over the Atlantic the swell builds up to an incredible height, trough to crest, and rolls in on Porthmeor in a smother of towering waves and foam. The new St. Ives motor lifeboat 'Caroline Parsons' rounded the Island on a falling tide, and with the rescue illuminated by the headlights of cars took off the 'Alba's' crew. But there was some delay in getting them aboard. As she cleared the wreck the lifeboat was dashed onto the sand by one receding wave, overwhelmed and capsized by the next, and slammed onto the Island rocks. The surf was alive with men flung into the sea, and struggling to grasp the outstretched hands of onlookers who now surged down to help. Although the wind was so stong that a man could scarcely keep to his feet against it, these helpers at great risk plucked all the lifeboatmen and most of the 'Alba's' seamen from that devil's cauldron. But five of the Hungarians were drowned.

In the calm of the next morning press and spectators arrived to view the battered 'Caroline Parsons' and the less obviously damaged freighter, high and dry and missing her funnel. But she too broke up and disappeared, in part beneath a camouflage of shellfish that blended her with the rocks.

That night of 31st January 1938 claimed a second victim, the old enemy rarely being sated with one. She was the 300 ton coaster 'Marena', of the County of Cornwall Steamship Company, and had been employed in carrying coal to the now defunct Hayle power station. Her stove-pipe smoke stack was a familiar sight in St. Ives Bay, and after thirty years of narrowly averted disaster she was known as the 'steam submarine.' She had gone aground three times in the last three years of her humble existence. But now, preoccupied as the town was with the 'Alba' rescue, no one was aware of her fate, no one came to her aid, and she met her doom alone.

If no one in St. Ives could forget 31st January 1938, too many have

St. Ives c. 1835

cause to remember and mourn the ancient fishing port's next lifeboat disaster. A week short of a year later, that ill-fated and for St. Ives doubly ill-fated year 1939, a Force 10 nor'-westerly had brewed up to 90 knots from Lands End to Newquay. At 2.30 a.m. of 23rd January St. Just coastguards reported a large steamship floundering under mountainous breakers two miles north of Cape Cornwall. Although the ship had not wirelessed an S.O.S. the coastguards contacted the West Cornwall lifeboats. The nearest, at Sennen, was immobile because the ebbing tide was almost clear of the slipway, but the St. Ives 'John and Sarah Eliza Stych' answered the call. Half an hour later she was battling through the breakers beyond Smeaton's Pier. Ninety volunteers had dragged the tons of boat and carriage, to which low water offered no obstacle that resolve, muscle and courage could not master, over the harbour sands and into the surf for launching. Several of them were injured when bowled over and swept under the carriage as they hauled waist deep, and chin deep as the tide surged, to float the boat.

The tide had now turned and was flooding into St. Ives Bay with the gale behind it, a raging sea which the 'John and Sarah Eliza Stych' met off the Island and made the best headway circumstances allowed abreast of Porthmeor Beach. Off Clodgy a 'seventh wave' bore down on her starboard bow and she capsized. Five lifeboatmen were thrown into the breakers, one retaining his grip on the lifeline until the boat righted herself and he was hauled back aboard. He was William Freeman. John Thomas the signalman was heard calling. His voice grew fainter until lost in the tumult. The four survivors restarted the engine, but a trailing rope fouled the propeller and wave, wind and tide drove the helpless lifeboat before them, not to be denied when the lifeboatmen dropped anchor off the Island and burned distress flares. The primeval powers of air and water snapped the stout Manilla cable like a thread and again overturned the boat. When she had righted, three of the eight were left. Beset by huge, tumbling seas the boat was hounded across St. Ives Bay and near the inner sound between the lighthouse and Godrevy Point capsized a third time. Now William Freeman, who had survived being flung overboard at Clodgy, was alone. It was 6.30 in the morning, four hours after the coastguard's call.

The 'John and Sarah Eliza Stych' was swept onto Godrevy rocks and left high and dry, as if inscrutable Providence had preserved William Freeman as witness to that night of terror. The lifeboatman's every move since the maroons roused St. Ives had been selective. He was not a regular member of the lifeboat crew, and had persuaded an older man who was ill and unfit to give him his place in the boat. He had been the one man to struggle back aboard when it capsized. Now he stepped out of the shattered lifeboat, scrambled up the cliff with every obstacle seeming as clear as by day to his quickened senses, and made his way through the frenzied dark to a nearby farmhouse. William Freeman lived on, an inspired though

Wreck of SS Alba, 1938. Wrecked Lifeboat in foreground.

broken man, to testify to the heroism of the lifeboat's crew, the frightful ordeal, the strength of the boat. He died on 23rd January 1978, on the thirty-ninth anniversary of the disaster.

Five of his seven crew-mates had been survivors of the 'Alba' rescue the previous January, for which they received gallantry medals from the R.N.L.I. President, H.R.H. the Duke of Kent. All the lifeboatmen who put to sea that dreadful night were married and related. They left eight young children, for whom the modest fruits of an appeal made some provision. The 1939 tragedy was the third occasion on which Coxswain Thomas Cocking had been flung into a violent sea when the lifeboat capsized. The body of this indomitable seaman - at 64 he would have been a few months off his pension today and marked for retirement - came ashore eight miles up the coast, at Portreath. Forty-four years a lifeboatman, and his cox'n's stipend - £16! These lifeboatmen give so much to the brotherhood of the sea - always their devotion, their skill, the hazard of their future, so often their lives.

As for the unknown freighter to the aid of which the 'John and Sarah Eliza Stych' had been summoned, she was - or is presumed to have been-the SS. 'Wilston', a 3,200 ton Glasgow tramp steamer bound for La Goulette, the port of Tunis, with Welsh coal and a crew of thirty. She was at first thought to have survived the gale and steamed away into the Atlantic, but daylight revealed wreckage on Wicca sands, eight miles east of where the steamship was reported in trouble off Cape Cornwall. Her steel hull, 335 feet (100 metres) from stem to stern, 48 feet in beam, had been flattened like a plastic toy under the foot of a child. Photographs taken that morning show her as little resembling a ship; rather a scatter of debris at the foot of the cliff. Investigation disclosed that her back must have been broken on the offshore rocks, from which the sea lifted her and dashed her broadside on the beach. There were no survivors. And as usual after hurricanes off the South West, bodies were washed ashore without any identification of ship or person.

Nor was the loss of the lifeboatmen unique in the history of St. Ives. In a November gale of 1803, thirty-seven years before the town had its first lifeboat, seven of the local fishermen manned a gig to row to the rescue of a Dutch East Indiaman's crew. The ship had been crippled by a Polperro privateer when war with Napoleon was renewed, and brought into St. Ives Bay. Barely was the gig clear of Smeaton's Pier when heavy seas capsized her. All seven lost their lives.

A happier episode resulted in all nine members of a St. Ives lifeboat crew receiving the first medals ever awarded for saving life from shipwreck. After a night of howling gale, the fury of which Hayle bar took in full blast, daybreak on 28th October 1865 revealed a vessel aground off Chapel Angier. This was, and is, an all too common spectacle for Hayle, and was a prime reason for the R.N.L.I.'s stationing a boat there the very next year and for fifty-four years to come. Now however it was the St. Ives boat that 'Down'long' St. Ives trundled on the cumbersome carriage into the breakers, for launching in a wild dash across the bay.

The wreck was the brig 'Providence' of Granville, on the west coast of the Normandy peninsula. Her crew of five clung to the rigging, while at their feet green seas surged clean over the hull, ever more menacing as flood tide and northerly gale in demonic alliance hurled the giant rollers at the harbour mouth. Abreast of the estuary Coxswain Nick Levett floated a 'drag-bag', a sea anchor, astern to steady the boat across the bar. She came in with two successive waves overtaking and rolling ahead. At the third the rope broke and she was swept onward at breakneck speed. An onlooker described how "she flew before the crest of the surf in an almost perpendicular position", then as the breaker cascaded upon the sandbank ran her bow under water and capsized. The lifeboat promptly righted herself, however, and all the lifeboatmen somehow scrambled back aboard and resumed their efforts. But with only four oars left progress was handicapped. When the valiant nine had got their boat under 'Providence's' lee, sea and current prevented their lying alongside.

Cox'n Levett then lay off while signalling the survivors in the rigging. They were to drift to the lifeboat, now to leeward of them, a rope lashed to a spar, and then make their way to the boat along the rope. It was an hour before the message was understood and acted upon. Then two of the Frenchmen essayed the daunting passage. One was dragged to safety, but as strong arms reached for the second man a tremendous sea overturned the lifeboat a second time. It righted instantly - a worthy boat indeed - and the crew and the first Frenchman were soon climbing back. The other was never seen again. The lifeboat again hauled up as close to the brig as storm and tide would allow, by which time the Captain and the remaining two had launched their own boat. No sooner had they cast off than it, too, capsized, flinging them into the surf. The lifeboat picked up all three, and brought them ashore, thus rescuing four out of five in circumstances that would have defeated all but the stoutest hearts.

Local subscriptions raised over £100 - a goodly sum in the 1860's - each lifeboatman receiving between £12 and £13. When news of the rescue reached France, Napoleon III, Emperor of the French, awarded "a gold medal of the First Class" to Coxswain Nicholas Levett, and a silver medal, First Class, to crewmen Paul Curnow, Thomas Veal, William Veal, Richard Curnow, Nathaniel Oliver, William Perkin Veal, Ishmael Job and John Blewett - as typical a selection of St. Ives names, these last eight, and all nine as gallant, as any in the annals of the ancient port. They were also awarded the first of the prized R.N.L.I. medals which were struck soon afterwards to acknowledge gallantry in rescue at sea.

1866 saw the inauguration of the Hayle Lifeboat Station. The boat, of the latest design, was presented by Oxford University and aptly named

'Isis.' She was a ten-oared boat and was housed in a quarry where until recently Esso have maintained a petrol depot, being launched by slipway into the harbour. Her send-off from Oxford was spectacular. Having drawn her through the streets of Oxford the undergraduates delivered her on the towpath to the 'Varsity Boat-Race eight, who had beaten Cambridge that year. After the naming ceremony by the Vice Chancellor's wife, the victorious crew rowed her up and down the river -a very different proposition from their own frail craft - and then to prove her qualities capsized her. No mean feat in such placid waters! With free transport from one railway system onto another the 'Isis' reached Hayle for a second grand procession, military band and escort and all.

'Isis' and her successors performed many brave rescues and saved a hundred or so lives, until in 1920 with the decline of shipping bound for Hayle the station was closed down. However vessels missing the narrow channel through fog or faulty navigation, or driven aground in a gale, were commonplace right up to the late 1970's. Then the sand was allowed, after so many centuries, undisputed possession of the only haven west of Padstow. Now there is nowhere to run for safety.

A very different St. Ives sea story concerns a small warship soon after World War II. On 30th September, 1952, when the wounds of Hitler's war were healing and that new threat to old ways, television, was moving in on Cornwall, a visitor in distress turned up at St. Ives and brought the whole town to her aid. A star overnight, she was reported and filmed and photographed and displayed throughout the South West. For early that Tuesday morning HMS 'Wave', a 950-ton minesweeper, loomed out of the wind and rain to plant herself solidly on the beach below the church.

The 'Wave', on Fishery Protection duty, had "come round the land", as they say of the sometimes hazardous trip from Newlyn to St. Ives, in a westerly gale and sought shelter in the lee of the Island. St. Ives Island, which has been a peninsula ever since man can remember, curves round the old town like a protecting arm, and there the 'Wave' rode at anchor through the night, snug and close to shore; dangerously close subsequent courts martial declared. But in that darkest hour before dawn the wind, veering, caught her in its full fury, as so many fine ships have been caught in St. Ives Bay.

At half past five on the morning of the 30th the duty Coastguard spotted that the 'Wave' was moving into danger. Her anchor chain had snapped, a most unusual occurrence and unobserved by the crew, who 'had their heads down.' The Coastguard flashed lamp signals. No response! He fired a maroon. Its warning was lost in the crash of the breakers. And the minesweeper was being buffeted into the shallows. Now lifeboat rockets boomed their starry summons into the first light of morning. St. Ives folk bounded out of bed, as always at the double thunder, an inborn expectancy of trouble triggering off instant activity. Hunched against the storm men and women streamed onto the wharf and the two piers and along the 'Lambeth Walk' to Westcott's Quay. The rocket brigade trundled the breeches buoy apparatus through the cobbled streets.

By now the 'Wave' was awake and noisy, but with no chance of avoiding the harbour beach. She grounded, shuddering at each blow of the sea but held fast in the sand as the tide ebbed. The rocket line was fired across her decks and secured, but it was decided to leave the crew on board; soon the whole ship would be on dry land! The 'Wave' was all lit up - just like Piccadilly, someone said - and when she was high and dry in the reluctant daylight naval men dropped down onto the beach and passed a cable to Smeaton's Pier to hold her off the rocks at the next tide. But the gale never abated. The ship floated, snapped the wire rope like a thread, and smashed onto Pednolver rocks.

One by one, and within a couple of hours, sixty-two of those of the ship's company who could be spared from duties aboard were hauled to Westcott's Quay by breeches buoy, through pounding seas and without serious injury, half the town helping and heaving. Oil gushed from the split hull, fouling the harbour and carried in slashing spray to bespatter the rescuers. And of course from the Salvation Army, ever the friend of sailors, came to a steady flow of tea and coffee.

At the next ebb the 'Wave' was found to be practically welded to the rocks with a gaping hole in her starboard side and her stern up against Westcott's Quay. A flotilla of salvage craft turned up from Plymouth, and the ship was relieved of all heavy gear. Forty-eight hours later the weather still stymied every attempt to get her off, until the Plymouth Harbour Master, Commander Brown, a seaman of vast experience and resource, had a barrage balloon stuffed into the hole and inflated from inside the hull. This did the trick! The 'Wave' lifted as the tide surged up over Pednolver rocks; sirens hooted and hawsers took the strain; the captain saluted the cheering crowd; and the minesweeper was hauled across the harbour to moorings alongside Smeaton's Pier.

First aid repairs; then the 'Wave', all £350,000's worth of her (but what would it be today?), sailed off for refit and further patrols, and the chase and arrest of law-breaking trawlers from Leningrad to Lisbon along our wild western shores.

In the 1850's, a hundred years before this episode, fishing by anybody and at any time (except in St. Ives on Sundays!) was no crime. What most occupied the forces of law and order then was smuggling, and the Crown was winning. The Royal Navy, no longer stretched to its limits against Napoleon, was scouring the seas, well-manned Revenue contingents watched the coast. But the Cornish coast is rugged and indented, with hundreds of little coves hard to discover even by day, and with clifftop tracks overgrown with furze and bramble, broken by landslides, impossible to follow at night. While on the clearest of days the

HMS Wave on Pednolva Rocks, St. Ives Harbour, 1952. From Richard Angove's Collection.

rim of the horizon beyond the land limits a masthead lookout's visibility to a twopenny-piece of ocean, the remainder of which might as well be hidden in darkest night for all he sees of it. So daring still paid dividends.

To this day they mention 'Old Worm's Fool' in St. Ives, though rarely now that the harbour more resembles a marina than a fishing port, while Down'long people are like as not immigrant English who set small store by nicknames, and whose traditions are of cornfields rather than coastlines. But 'Old Worm' does crop up from time to time, when you may gather that to be his fool is almost a term of respect, a tribute to acting stupid while knowing all.

Who, then, were Old Worm and his fool? To meet them as they were is to step back into the St. Ives of nearly a century and a half ago, a St. Ives at first glance recognisable as today's, at the second, much different. No promenade encircled the harbour, Smeaton's great granite pier stopped short at the squat lighthouse now halfway along its added length, there was no West Pier at all. The shops were mostly in Fore Street. The main road squeezed between church and market house, crawled steeply up Skidden Hill, continued as breathlessly up to the Belyars, and levelled out through Tregenna woods. The harbour foreshore was noisy with shipbuilding. And however tightly the port might be packed when the fishing fleet heaved home to discharge its catch on the sands at low tide, vessels from the Continent, from Ireland, from the Americas yet found a space to moor amid the tangle of chains and the forest of masts. The business of the town was largely in fish, and it smelt so, and much of its needs was seaborne too. And while bales and baskets and barrels crowded the wharf and were carted away throughout the busy day there were nights when casks, and those smallish, slab-sided kegs called ankers, were toted ashore to vanish mysteriously and with as little fuss as the day-time trade had been all bustle and hullabaloo.

For sheer, cool daring few smugglers could equal Captain James Williams of St. Ives, whose ubiquitous patronym was necessarily distinguished by a nickname, his for one reason or another being 'Old Worm.' His most notorious exploit occurred in the early summer of 1851. He had brought his smack 'St. George' in among the crowded shipping with a cargo of whisky from Ireland - a cargo he had no intention of declaring to Her Majesty's Customs and Excise. This he distributed where there was least likelihood of discovery to await dispersal. Some disappeared into fishing boats laid up for overhaul, the rest going to 'Pigs' Town.' Pigs' Town was an enclosure behind the wharf where the smell of the sties in summer stifled even that of the fish, and was not to be approached save at need.

On the last night of May month Old Worm made his move. There were orders to meet up Redruth way, where the gentry and such would fancy a change from brandy, while with tin booming the miners had a shilling or two to spend. Judging that the hour was so late as to have seen the last of the lawmen abed, Captain Williams and his crew launched a couple of waggons loaded with whisky onto the cobblestones, and with clumping hooves and rumble of wheels set off up Fore Street.

But Old Worm had reckoned without the propensity of Coastguard Cock - the coastguards were the backbone of the land-based 'Preventives' - for making the most of the 'one for the road.' This officer was still sipping his cordial (on which, we trust, full duty had been paid!) at the George and Dragon in Market Place when the clatter brought him out of the taproom and into the street - to be promptly knocked down, bound and gagged by Old Worm himself and one of his men. They left him in the gutter and hurried on through the lonely night. Extra horses were standing by to be hitched to the waggons for the haul up Skidden Hill, and by the time the hapless Cock had worked free of his bonds and reported to the Coastguard Commander, who lived in the Warren, the smugglers were well on their way. The commander climbed into his saddle and spurred off in pursuit. On Hayle Causeway the toll house keeper, his pockets heavy with Old Worm's bribe, swore that neither man nor beast had passed by, whereupon the commander galloped off to Penzance. Meanwhile his quarry was urging the steaming nags in the opposite direction through Hayle, then Camborne, and at last Redruth, where the whisky was delivered and the smugglers went to ground.

Fooled, but not 'Old Worm's Fools', the Revenue Officers turned their furious attentions upon Captain Williams's smack 'St. George', a fully decked sloop well suited to the legitimate coastal trade under cover of which James Williams conducted his 'free trading' activities. They boarded her with all the elan one would expect of the Preventive Service in full cry, with a watertight case and a rascally crew sleeping off the night's exertions below, ripe for the plucking. Instead they found one bewildered German lad rubbing the sleep from his eyes, in sole charge of a ship from which every shred of evidence had long been removed.

This young seaman, who was known as Prussian Bob, had signed on with Captain Williams at Bristol, the smack's port of registry, after running away to sea from his home at Memel. Bob was questioned for hours, though without the forceful persuasion, one assumes, which would have been his lot in his fatherland, but the officers were no wiser at noon than they had been at sunrise. In English the fellow didn't know, in German he couldn't be understood. Loyalty, and perhaps the threat of a rope's end, had ensured his giving nothing away. The boy was a fool, the disgruntled Excisemen concluded; 'Old Worm's Fool.'

The 'St. George' was arrested, on a trivial charge for lack of evidence. Captain Old Worm Williams returned from completing his affairs at Redruth to whip up that public sympathy which habitually supported the defendant in smuggling cases. In a letter to the press he claimed that Coastguard Cock had emerged from the pub in the dark to be accidentally run down by a passing waggon, which he had imagined in tipsy confusion to be feloniously employed. Shame that the unwarranted suspicions of a drunkard should so jeopardise an honest mariner's livelihood as to drive him to beg his bread in his native town, while his crew starved!

The letter did the trick. Prussian Bob's professions of ignorance remained unshaken, no proof was offered either to confirm the charge of smuggling or to clear the hapless Cock, and on instructions from headquarters the charge was dropped. And the German seaman? After a successful career with Captain Williams during which he learnt enough English, at any rate of the St. Ives blend, vintage 1850's, to get by, he retired on the profits of the moonshine trade to become a noteworthy citizen of the Cornish seaport and be respectfully known, then and for generations to come, as 'Old Worm's Fool.'

Trevail Cove is off the beaten track nowadays and from a conservationist viewpoint mercifully forgotten. But a picnic there was a favourite outing for St. Ives folk in those summers of the 'twenties and 'thirties from which memory sorts out the golden days and dismisses the dross. Baskets bulging with pasties and saffron and 'hevva' cake, and splits and pots of cream and strawberry jam or treacle, and the youngest of the party swinging the tin kettle, you tramped joyously up the Stennack. From the Zennor road you deviated seawards, through fields and heathered moorland to the cliff path, thence to descend adventurously to the cove. Otherwise you plodded further along the highway between Rosewall and Buttermilk hills, diverged into lanes growing even narrower and through hamlets that are pure ancient Celtic in origin, passed a derelict mill beside Trevail Farm, and plunged into tracks where gorse and bracken crowded in on you until you emerged as from a tunnel into the lovely cove.

This narrow inlet with its beach inviting at low tide and no one about but yourselves was ideal for a picnic; and if you struggled home in the moonlight desperately tired, it was worth it. Walking was as commonplace then as driving is today, when so many new roads lead right up to spots which have shed romance with remoteness. But Trevail stays unsullied. Access is overgrown and difficult, though once arrived you would find no better haven for a day's idling. Or, had you been an early Victorian rather than a latter day Elizabethan, for smuggling.

In the 1840's a smuggler named Trevaskis was known for his success in eluding the law. He had an eye for out of the way landings for his contraband, and as importantly for hideouts until the coast should be clear for distribution inland. Thus it was that in the Spring of 1846 he chose Trevail for a 'run' and asked the miller at the grist mill if he might leave some property on the premises for a week or two. The miller, a 'born innocent' to whom the smuggler was a complete stranger, acquiesced.

The George & Dragon Inn, Market Place, St. Ives c. 1900. Here Portreeve John Payne had his last meal before hanging in the Market Place outside. Courtesy Royal Institute of Cornwall.

Whereupon in due course a file of men tramped up from the cove while the mill slept, each with an anker under either arm or a keg slung on his shoulder, and dumped the load at a furze rick in one of the miller's fields. There Trevaskis with practised skill concealed his haul. And there an excise officer with a nose for hideaways found it.

The miller, who valued his reputation beyond all things else and dreaded the court case which would disclose his complicity in a crime, named Trevaskis but bribed the exciseman to drop all reference to himself. This cost him his life's savings, £200 in all and the then considerable fortune which you would expect of an industrious old miller with his golden thumb.

The corrupt officer tracked down Trevaskis and offered him like terms. Trevaskis, though, was not going to pay bribes to a danged exciseman, not on his life he wasn't! So off his aggrieved captor took him for Bodmin Assizes. The two boarded the train at Hayle station (this was still to be seen until recently, beneath the viaduct where the road makes a U-bend at Foundry) and were to change to another line at Redruth. The railway skirted the further side of Hayle Pool and crossed to Angarrack. The incline there was so steep that the trains had to be connected to a cable and winched up Steamer's Hill by a stationary engine which gave the place its name. On this very occasion, 1st June 1846, the Hayle Railway suffered its one major accident - an occasion you may consider should have met with better fortune, for the 11 a.m. for Redruth carried not only a felon being haled to judgement, but nine coachloads of Methodists bound for the annual Whit Monday Wesley service at Gwennap Pit. Near the top of the hill a coupling broke and the last four coaches, all open carriages at the cheaper fare and crammed with a hundred and thirty people, careered backwards with ever increasing momentum. Many of the terrified passengers jumped out, some were injured. One was killed; the exciseman. Trevaskis picked himself up and made off home, none the worse, to resume his nefarious trade.

Meanwhile the miller, the innocent victim of this lucky villain, had been persistently nagged by his wife - and who can blame her? - for his stupidity in getting involved with a smuggler and in parting so readily with their nest-egg. Now added to her upraidings was the grievance that Trevaskis should have got off scot free while it was herself and her poor simpleton who suffered. It was all too much for the old man. He hanged himself in the mill.

One sunny day in the summer of 1916, when West Cornwall lanes drowsed in a contentment of leaf and blossom, when shocks of corn dotted the fresh stubble, and skylarks trilled and levitated above the moors with such an illusion of peace that you could forget Flander's Fields, the depths where U-boats lurked, and the whole bloody business of war, a two-horse waggonette set forth from St. Ives for Gurnard's Head. Gurnard's Head, beyond Zennor and the last promontory before Pendeen Light, quite resembles the big-headed fish from which its name derives. It is one of those natural, rock-crowned fastnesses that jut well out into the Cornish sea, and is a tourist attraction well worth a visit; a coastal feature of outstanding grandeur and good, weather permitting, for a picnic and a laze in the sun. Which is what Mr. W.J. Jacobs had in mind when he loaded family and friends, a dozen in all, aboard the vehicle. The late 'W.J.' was editor of the St. Ives newspaper 'Western Echo' (now incorporated in the 'Times & Echo' and 'Hayle Times'), and it is from his private journal, and his daughter Mary's vivid recollection of the occasion, that this tale of the coast has with her consent been culled.

The picnickers dismounted at the inn and made their merry way down the footpath towards the Head. The place seemed deserted. Much of West Cornwall was yet to be 'discovered' by holiday-makers, while in wartime Gurnard's Head was scarcely more frequented than when, a hundred years previously, the 'rider' of the Excise had made his solitary rounds. After the shoulder-to-shoulder life of the busy fishing port such isolation was delightful. The little knot of people in this emptiness of cliff and sky comprised, besides Mr. and Mrs. Jacobs and their little girls Kitty and Mary, Messrs. Seaman and Craze, the Lukes, brother-in-law Harvey Toy, who was a chief officer of the Hain Steamship Company home on leave, and one or two others not distinguishable in the V.P.K. (Vest Pocket Kodak) snapshot that commemorates this outing.

The path skirted fields which slanted ever more steeply until at the neck of the headland they were but a ferny, furzey, boulder-strewn tumbledown to the sea. But what was keeping W.J.? They looked back and saw him in earnest conversation with a man in uniform, whom you might have imagined, so unexpected his appearance, to be the exciseman back on his beat again. And so, in a way, he was. He was a Coast Watcher, an auxiliary Coastguard, whom Mary recognised as an acquaintance of her father's. Trouble? Charles Seaman, a schoolmaster with that sense of public accountability which goes with the job, would go back and see. The rest must carry on; they'd catch up with them later.

A field further on the corn had been cut, the 'neck cried', and the sheaves stacked high to await the harvest home. There the party, strung out with their baskets of sandwiches and saffron cake and those new-fangled vacuum flasks that obviated the sooty, if jolly, chore of boiling the water on a furze fire, and chattering in mutually exclusive twos and threes, froze, slowed, bunched and stared. For stretched out in the shade of the corn-shocks lay three men, strangers, strangely dressed. One looking up tried to hide a suitcase under the raincoat he lay on. The others slept.

"What funny clothes!" said Mary.

"I've seen 'em dressed like that in Hamburg," observed Uncle Harvey the sailor. In those early years of the century everyday dress had not surrendered national characteristics to the uniformity induced by travel, press photography and T.V.

Germans! Never! The party moved on, not giving them another thought - all except Mary. Mary felt that the sunshine was fading out of her day.

Meanwhile Mr. W.J. Jacobs, journalist and editor, was getting a story he could not use and a command he could not refuse. His journal records that the Coast Watcher told him, "I have just come up from the headland and on walking through the second field away from here, where there are some corn stacks, I saw three or four men lying down asleep. They looked to me like Germans. But I have an appointment to meet another coast watcher two miles away in half an hour's time, and I must keep that appointment. I want you to go down to the coastguard station and report this matter."

"At first (writes W.J.) I suggested that the Coast Watcher would be better employed keeping his eye on the Germans, but this he refused to do. So I went to the coastguard station. This took me away to the right from our party. There after much knocking and shouting a coastguard came to meet me and asked my business. I told him. He seemed very agitated and said, 'I cannot do anything about it. My mate has gone to Penzance for the afternoon, and I am alone in the station, and for all I know you yourself may be a German.'

This appalling comment, coming as it did on top of the refusal of those representatives of H.M. services who were on the spot to tangle with the foe, stirred W.J., a stubborn but not aggressive man and no giant withal, to stand his ground. The argument was reaching ignition point when Charles Seaman hove in sight and was promptly hailed by his friend. Together they roused the reluctant custodian of the coast to action. They, decreed the coastguard, were to advance and challenge the presumed enemy while from the station he covered them with the rifle provided for such an emergency. This was not a plan of campaign that won unanimous approval. They would not go unless the coastguard went too. But no, he could not leave his post. His subordinate, mused W.J., could not stay, he could not leave!

The two friends thereupon hurried apprehensively across the field to join the others and tell their alarming story. Imagine their surprise when they learnt that the picnic party, too, had spotted the strangers, and that Harvey had identified them as Germans. Now Mr. Craze took charge. His son had lost a leg on the field of battle, and he himself had from the first entertained doubts as to proceeding with the jollifications while the emissaries of Kaiser Wilhelm went about their fiendish machinations nearby. He pointed out so vehemently where their duty lay that the whole party turned back, not straggling as before, but in the closest order possible, to flush out the foe. The armed forces of the Crown might funk it,

Botallack Mine next to the ill-fated Levant.

but they were cast in sterner mould.

As they retraced their steps along the footpath the coastguard came charging across the fields flourishing a rifle. His mate had returned from Penzance, and orders were that the picnickers were to search the area and arrest the strangers. Reinforced by the professional and supported by the artillery, the gallant band felt invincible. But the reinforcement was not to be. Mary remembers his thrusting the weapon into someone's hand - Uncle Harvey's, she believes - and while the coastguard directed from the rear, like army HQ across the Channel, off they stole among the shocks. However, you will hardly wonder that by now "the birds had flown. The coastguard seemed at a loss to know what to do. We went up to the hotel and found that a group of young fellows similar to those for whom we were looking had recently left in a conveyance and gone in the direction of Penzance. I therefore suggested to the coastguard that he telephone to all coastguard stations, also the police, in the vicinity and warn them.

"Whatever happened I never knew, but I do remember hearing that German submarine crews had boasted to British sailors that they had been ashore and stayed at a Penzance hotel."

German submariners?

Some local folk still persist, despite all denial, that the famous author and his German wife who then lived at Zennor were in touch with the enemy. Well, he never got on with the natives, nor they with him. At about this time two children discovered a cache of oil drums in a cave at Carbis Bay, but were too scared to report it. And everybody knew that World War I U-boats used to put in at Prussia Cove, the smugglers' stronghold in Mounts Bay, to refuel......

It is a wild, wild coast, where so much has transpired of which we shall never hear tell. And only of late has the holiday world trodden every track, explored each accessible cave. What do you think?

CHAPTER EIGHT

SAILORS' RETURN, & THE MAN-ENGINE

How, we have wondered who never knew imprisonment with its clanging of doors and grating of keys, the bullying of guards and the interminable togetherness of fellow captives - how did the prisoners of war in World Wars I and II endure it, some of them for over six years? We rejoiced in their escapes, even - in retrospect - when it had been from our own compounds, admired their persistence when they tried again. Meet then Thomas Williams of St. Ives, captured at sea in 1804, confined in French gaols as a boy, escaped three times only to be retaken, and returned to his native land in 1814 on the fall of the Emperor Napoleon. Ten years of brutal confinement, with no Geneva Convention to shelter him as in the Europe of the 1900's, no Red Cross to intervene, while the lad grew to manhood!

Thirteen-year-old Tom Williams had been a boy-seaman in the merchant brig 'Friendship' when in late March, 1804, she loaded stores at a London wharf for Devonport dockyard and then proceeded to the Downs in the Thames estuary. Here during the Napoleonic war convoys assembled for the perilous voyage down the French coast, where privateers (Nelson did not distinguish them from pirates, on whichever side they plundered) were alert in a dozen sea-ports to cut out prizes which had straggled beyond the protection of the Royal Navy's escorts.

The convoy, waiting perhaps a week or more for the wind that would speed it past Ushant and into the open Atlantic, weighed anchor as soon as it blew, the order being given by the senior officer of the escort. When the signal flags had fluttered up to the naval mastheads, the ratlines would swarm with men mounting aloft, many for the first and most frightening time in their lives. As the cables clanked home far below, great white sails fell into place from the yards and were hauled taut, if not so smartly as when, before the next port of call, the newly press-ganged recruits had been drilled into shape.

Light naval units careered among the merchantmen, chivvying and exhorting until their seamen, too, were shoving against the capstan bars, bare feet slapping the deck round and round to the rhythm of a chanty, and the cable snaked aboard dripping and oozing Thames slime. Brass lunged mates with brass-bound speaking trumpets would roar commands in tones that had out-thundered hurricanes. Then with sail enough to give headway the convoy would move off the anchorage and away from the Downs to the chance encounters of war and the certain hazards of the sea.

It was to be expected that the favourable wind which sprang up to urge the convoy down-Channel would isolate some slow starter or other from the rest. Accordingly fast French sloops and luggers would hover off the North Foreland or even further up the estuary to snatch a straggler scurrying like a tail-end duckling to join the flock. Which was what befell the brig 'Friendship.' She had dallied too long on the Downs, to pick up a new longboat. In the night of 28th March, as she made her best speed - it could never be termed fast - to catch up with the convoy, young Tom on foc's'l lookout reported a lugger bearing down on them "on a wind." It disappeared in the darkness, then was seen approaching from astern. A hail got no reply. Grapnels were thrown, French privateersmen came aboard in a terrifying rush over the counter, and the brig was seized. They took her into Dieppe, where the crew were stripped of everything but the clothes they wore and flung into the dungeon of the local castle.

On 1st April Tom and his shipmates began their march of fifteen to twenty miles a day to Givet, on the north-east frontier. It took fourteen exhausting, underfed days to get there, and was a prelude to seven years of boredom and misery for the St. Ives lad, longer for most of his comrades. They were confined in a cavalry barrack, with exercise mornings only, three roll calls a day, and starvation diet. With them at Givet were the ships' companies of two British warships that had run aground while patrolling the enemy coast, and of a Royal Mail Packet caught in French waters at the renewed outbreak of war the year before. Tom whiled away the hungry hours by renewing his studies, in the course of which he discovered in himself an interest in and aptitude for mathematics, and thence for navigation. With only one manual amongst them, Tom copied out all the nautical tables in it, and in time became so proficient that he gave lessons in navigation to others. The odd sou thus earned supplemented his daily allowance of three farthings (less deductions) and went to meet a growing youth's need for food. After four years the allowance increased by an extra farthing made all the difference between starvation and survival.

Seven despairing years crept by at Givet, with hope of exchange for French prisoners in England dwindling as each March gone passed into another April. Thought of escape grew paramount. Others had tried but failed, and being caught were beaten severely. Two midshipmen who got away were cornered in a cave. A blast of gunfire killed one of them, the other was mercilessly cut down as, unarmed and helpless, he ran out. There was no 'underground' to help escapers, no real life Scarlet Pimpernel to snatch you from Napoleon's secret police. Tom Williams had tried on several occasions to slip past the guards, but their vigilance by day and night had defeated him. A last in March 1811, almost seven years to the day since the 'Friendship' fell to a privateer on the Downs, with two of his shipmates he made it. How this difficult and dangerous feat was accomplished the confused manuscript (abridged and reproduced by Matthews) which relates Tom's adventures makes no mention. The clue probably lies in his later escapes through a hole in the wall, and next by burrowing - "like one little mouse" as an examining magistrate gleefully observed. But of course tunnelling is inbred in a race of which it has been said, "wherever in the world there's a hole in the ground, you will find a Cornishman at the bottom of it!"

Liberty lasted for four days. Then recapture, court martial, and sentence. A brutal sentence. Six years' imprisonment in irons. Six more years not as prisoners of war, but as condemned criminals, with the added savagery of fetters to be removed only after almost as long again as their previous incarceration, should they live that long; of dragging heavy iron shackles between chafed ankles as they laboured by day, and at night padlocked to the wall of the filthy den in which they would exist like a bear dedicated, poor beast, to the current sport of bear-baiting, and with scarcely more hope of survival.

But as Tom and his companions despaired, Lady Luck spared them a smile. While they waited in the county gaol for their transfer to the prison and shackles decreed for them, Marie Louise, Napoleon's new Empress, bore a son and the Emperor proclaimed an amnesty in baby Napoleon II's honour. Pardons signed by His Imperial Majesty himself were publicly presented to the three sailors, and reverting to their P.O.W. status they were marched back to Givet. There they were kept in close confinement, to await yet again orders as to their disposal. Fearing that the imperial police, thwarted by an unwanted act of clemency, would be all the more resolved to keep them within their claws, they got to work on their cell wall and burrowed through it. For the second time since that night on the Downs Tom Williams was a free man. He was then twenty-two.

The three escapers soon came to a house in a wood. Thinking it to be a farmhouse, and desperate for food, they knocked on the door. A gamekeeper lived there, the walls bristling with the weaponry of his calling. He was a rough, burly fellow, they were wan and famished, but they compelled him to boil them some bread and milk, after which they went off into the night. Next morning they came to a village which turned out to have been "the brave old Duke of York's" headquarters early in the war, when he marched his ten thousand men "up to the top of the hill and marched them down again." The British regiments must have made a good name for themselves, for the villagers treated Tom and his friends well.

You will recall that Givet was a town near the north east frontier -in French Flanders where there are so many "corners of a foreign field that are for ever England." Journeying by night they reached the sea between Ostend and Nieuport in eleven days. They steered principally by the North Star and "the comet", which appeared on their "N.W. quarter" and must have been Pon's comet, on view in September 1812 -an indication of how the years were creeping by. You can imagine the sailors' delight at the sniff of brine in the wind, the glint of wave-crests under the stars, the confident expectation of finding a boat, launching it from the beach, and sailing home. But no boat could be found. They worked their way down the coast, sustaining themselves by calling at isolated cottages on the way. Dusk was the best time for such a call, for one reason or another fewer men being then at home. Tom would go indoors while the others kept watch outside and persuade the family to give them a meal. Likely enough Tom was a personable young man whose looks appealed to madame and ma'amselle alike. But should entreaties fail the others came in and they helped themselves. They crossed one river with Tom, who could not swim, using a gate for a raft while his mates swam alongside, pushing it. Then they called at a farmhouse, where the farmer put them into his barn, doubtless balancing the shortage of sturdy farm-hands, all conscripted into Napoleon's armies, against the treasonable but eminently desirable employment of the three Britishers. His wife weighed in with care and kindliness too, and "I might have stayed there for good", wrote Tom, "but I had my native land in view."

They reached the outskirts of Dunkirk; still no boat. There a householder, hostile at first, turned out to be a good friend. After spending a couple of nights with him, warm and well fed, they confessed that they were Englishmen. At this he informed them - surely to their surprise - that a number of English vessels were moored in Dunkirk harbour, and they could expect a quick passage home. Since they were still wearing ragged prison clothes they feared that they would not get past the sentries at the drawbridges on the ramparts. So Tom wrote a letter describing their predicament and calling their fellow countrymen to their aid, and their host, donning his go-to-meeting clothes, took it into town. There he met several English shipmasters in a tavern. After a lengthy debate over Tom's letters, in English which the Frenchman could not follow, they refused either to help or even to visit the escaped prisoners. Their reason, you may suppose, was that Dunkirk though French was a free port, an international market place in which strictest neutrality must be observed.

A poor reason, though, for prisoners of war on the run. They shook off the dust of their shoes against Dunkirk, so to speak, and plodded along the shore towards Boulogne. Who would declare himself English any more after such treatment by his own folk? They would pass themselves off as American seamen in search of a berth. Arriving at Boulogne after dark, they were stopped by sentries so agreed to lie low until daybreak, when they could inconspicuously join the crowds surging through the city gates. But at dawn they discovered to their horror that they had settled down for the night within a French army camp, teeming with troops. Escape was impossible, so they followed some 'poilus' through a breach in the ramparts. Nobody challenged them; they were in the town, and soon on the quay, which was coming to life for a new day's toil. And the stars and stripes flapped in the breeze from ships at moorings. Their pilgrimage, with its hardships and hazards, its hopes and disappointments, was almost at an end.

Or so they thought.

Entering a tavern to fortify themselves with wine and a meal before presenting themselves to a prospective employer, they discussed their intention with the landlady. As soon as it was reasonable for a good Christian man to be out of bed, she told them, she would herself call on an American shipowner in the neighbourhood and bring him along to interview them. Meanwhile they must relax and enjoy their breakfast. Presently she left them, to return with - armed gendarmes. The game was up! They were handcuffed and once more flung into the town gaol.

Boulogne gaol accommodated at the time, besides the three Britons, a senile Welshman and a horde of giant rats, a hundred or more army and navy deserters, all herded together in an underground cell. The old Welshman, to whom Tom and his mates naturally gravitated, had come to France during the Peace (1801-'3) to instruct the French in coal mining. In his declining years he longed for the Valleys and applied for passage home. This was refused, whereupon he made himself a canvas boat. It being too heavy to handle alone, he hired a woman to bear a hand. They were however arrested before the old man could launch it, and he had rotted in prison ever since.

Nights passed badly. Incessant bantering between soldiers and sailors, rival choruses bellowed simultaneously, held sleep at bay. But the days were worse. The daily ration was one pound of brown bread and some soup. This consisted of cabbage, a few potatoes, and a little bread, served steaming hot in a large kettle to each group of ten. Each man had a wooden spoon, which he dipped into the brew in turn. Should you spoon up a potato you were sure to lose your next turn or two, the potato being too hot to swallow at a gulp. Meat was served once in the ten days that Tom spent there. In the general scramble which followed its appearance he fared ill. Marching orders were welcome, though as the narrative does not mention Tom's shipmates thereafter, it seems he went alone.

Tom was committed to the citadel of Briancon in the Alps. At first in a "bomb-proof room" he then, presumably for some misdemeanour, spent a month in a dark subterranean cell. The last fifteen days of this he passed, as you would expect of a 'Cousin Jack', tunnelling his way to freedom. He was recaptured on the mountains, in the shadow of Mont Blanc, and made to march, chained to other prisoners with a French army across the Alps. But the rule of the Emperor Napoleon I came to an end, at any rate for a year, in March 1814 - a fateful month for Tom Williams too. Napoleon abdicated and was banished to the Isle of Elba. Tom Williams on 14th May landed at Mousehole and walked home to St. Ives, where his mother did not know him. But how should she recognise in the burly sailorman the boy who had kissed her goodbye ten long years ago? He never went to sea again, but opened a school in St. Ives and became parish clerk. Tom died in 1862 at the fair old age of seventy-one, the deprivations and hardships of his boyhood seeming to have done him little harm. But perhaps he was a tyrant of a schoolmaster; or had the persecutions of his own youth rendered him gentler to the duffer in the back row than was common in the insensitive Victorian age?

Carn Glaze house is the oldest house in St. Ives; the wall tablet tells you so. Opposite the car-park behind the Sloop Inn it was formerly faced by a huddle of tenements, some containing bedrooms without windows, which was pulled down in the 1930's in the interest of public health, for all that people lived there to advanced old age. J.H. Matthews, whose 'History of St. Ives, Lelant, Towednack and Zennor' is every subsequent St. Ives historian's bible, concluded that Carn Glaze is the 'Ugnes' house mentioned in the archives, where Hugenot refugees were accommodated at public expense throughout the seventeenth century.

These French Protestants, bearing such names as Bourdeaux, Ruffignac, Du Toit (Toy) still known in Cornwall, had been driven from their homeland by Catholic persecution. However at the close of the century Mayor Hicks leased the house to a Reginald Botterall who, though of French extraction, was no Hugenot but of far more ancient ancestry. The Bottrells, to use the current spelling of their variously rendered but unmistakeable name, are of baronial Breton stock who followed William the Conqueror to England in 1066. Various estates granted to them in Cornwall (there were others over the country but they settled here) included "Bottreaux Castle, seated on a bad harbour of the north sea" (this was Boscastle) "and suburbed with a poor market town, yet entitling the owner in times past with the style of a Baron." So comments the Cornish Elizabethan Richard Carew! Among their Cornish holdings were Bosworgy at St. Erth and the manor of Lelant and Trevethoe.

Despite the decline of family fortunes during, though probably not because of, the Wars of the Roses, the Bottrells flourish to this day, the Christian names William and Reginald running through the whole long line of them. The Victorian writer who ensured the immortality of West Cornish folk lore in his "Traditions and Hearthside Stories" was a William Bottrell. He lived for a while at Hawks Point, Carbis Bay.

The Reginald Botterall who occupied Carn Glaze in 1699 was a sea captain. He returned to the house about a hundred and thirty years later, appearing on the steps that led to a side door of the big room there and described as "a ruddy-faced, pleasant-looking, stout little gentleman...... his belly round and tight as a drum." This apparition was attested by two brothers, Ephraim the elder, and Tom aged twelve, who told J.H. Matthews the story long afterwards, when perhaps memory and fantasy had joined forces. For fisherman Tom (who would not allow his surname to be published) gave a singularly detailed description of this agreeable phantom. The late Captain Botterall had sported "a long cut-away coat, long black velvet waistcoat, black breeches of the same material, black ribbed stockings, and pump shoes tied with a bow ribbon. His head was bald, save for a small bit of hair at the back, and he had no hat. Brass or gold buttons adorned his coat and waistcoat, on the latter two rows. The buttons of his coat were embossed in the centre in the shape of flowers." Tom gazed spell-bound at the stout little gentleman for a minute, and when he vanished woke his brother, who had fallen asleep, and told him all about it. Relating this experience to the rest of the family on their return from visiting, they were laughed at. Nevertheless they all left Carn Glaze soon afterwards, though whether the jolly captain was doing his rounds again, or is to be met with now, is not recorded. Such a nice old ghost! Keep your eyes open.

The old fifteenth century Market House, demolished and rebuilt in 1832, suffered supernatural visitations we are better without. Immediately overlooking the George and Dragon Inn it had a window to which ghost-layers, who earned a pretty shilling or two by securing the living from the assaults of the dead, used to consign troublesome spirits. It seems that exorcism, which today is practised somewhat roughly on the persons of the possessed, was then applied with like vigour to those from beyond the grave whose ravings (mercifully no longer on our wave-length) annoyed the worthy citizens of James Wallis's day. James Wallis, a respected if feared exorcist of two hundred years ago, and the last of the professional ghost-layers, did the job after dark with book and candle while his apprentice, who apparently did not serve his time, rang the bell. A brave lad! For another, who witnessed this preliminary skirmish with the departed, ran like a hare and so deprives us of an interesting instruction. One gathers that a ghost-layer frequently bound and belaboured his adversary; though how to tell where you had got him and how to hit him must have been a secret of the craft.

It is on record that the ghostly reprobates James Wallis and his predecessors had bundled through the Market House window made a most unholy row. And when you recall that stocks and whipping posts then stood in the Market Place outside; that a cage for exhibiting criminals had formerly swung there too; and that it had been opposite the George and Dragon, in the aftermath of the Cornish Rebellion of 1538, that John Payne, Portreeve of St. Ives, had been hanged as "a busy rebel" after entertaining King's Commissioner Kingston at the inn and ordering the erection of the gallows to oblige the fellow, what can you expect at such an accursed spot but outbursts of spectral indignation?

There is no cause to falter, though, as you pick your way through Market Place nowadays. The George and Dragon has long since gone the way of the old Market House, while the present building, opened in the hopeful year of parliamentary reform and its upper floor courthouse no more the scourge of miscreants, is a nuisance, albeit a picturesque one, to nothing but the traffic.

Snug in bed with the first 'cuppa' of the day, we used to follow Radio 4's 'Coastal Footpath' week by week on 'Morning Sou' West', with Bill Best Harris, Plymouth librarian turned intrepid explorer, to talk us along. Better still, walk that section of the footpath towards Cape Cornwall from Gurnard's head, where the German agents had made so accommodated a landing. However your ramble may more nearly resemble a safari than a summer stroll, it will reward you with some of the most enchanting scenery you ever saw. Half way on you will come to Geevor mine, also attainable, if less dramatically, by major roads from both St. Ives and Penzance. Geevor is a modernised tin mine with headgear that would look sophisticated in the newest Nottinghamshire coalfield. It adjoins - is almost entangled with - the old Levant mine, where tinners were burrowing long before up-country colliers had exploited their own green pastures and the crowding forests of England. Levant surface workings extend to the cliff edge and continue down the cliff face. What sort of men were these 'Cousin Jacks', you wonder, who with block and tackle, clumsy timber scaffolding and indomitable persistence built so dizzily in wind and weather?

Geevor, which still survives the fluctuating fortunes of tin mining, incorporates many of the underground workings of the Levant. Dr. A.K. Hamilton Jenkin, the miners' historian, being conducted through half forgotten labyrinths in the 1920's, saw by the glimmer of his candle "K.1790" cut into the tunnel wall; some tinner's enduring memorial hidden away in the deep dark. The Levant had failed at the turn of the century, but after a false start in 1810 was reopened ten years later. The new company struck a rich lode of copper near the surface that paid for sinking a shaft to one of the deepest levels in Cornwall, and driving its galleries far out under the sea.

At about the time of Queen Victoria's accession the 'man-engine' was introduced to Cornish mines. You might imagine from its somewhat harsh name that this was no less a feature of the nastier side of Victorian life than man-traps and treadmills. In fact it was in its day a blessing, immeasurably lightening the labours of our tinners. Until its invention the Cornish miner had to climb, usually vertically, a thousand feet of ladders or more before the start or at the finish of a 'core' (= shift), the day's work covering only the time spent on the actual job. Think of it -down rung by unequal rung into a darkness not to be assessed by the dark of the blackest night, the narrow shaft close about you, your only light the candle stuck by a lump of clay onto your hard felt hat, and those of your mates above and below, all stomping down into the bowels of the earth! Then there was the long walk to the 'pitch', at which with fellow 'tributers' you slogged through a six or eight-hour core. This over there was the climb 'to grass' with the pick and shovel you never let go of. After that you tramped perhaps several miles home through day or night in every kind of weather. A tough life, a demanding life, rarely extending beyond fifty years. Yet a tinner was proud of his strength and endurance; would not change places with a longer living farm-hand who earned less, and was far less independent, than himself.

In 1841 a prize was offered for an efficient alternative to ladders. It was won by a famous engineer, Michael Loam. His invention was the Man-Engine. This was a device by which a series of twelve-foot lengths of timber, joined end to end by metal plates, extended from top to bottom of a steeply slanting or vertical shaft. At surface a steam engine, housed in one of those massive granite buildings you see crumbling into romantic ivied ruin all over Cornwall, lifted this enormous length of 'rods' up twelve feet, then at the next turn of the wheel lowered it back. Sometimes two lengths of rods ran side by side, one rising as the other fell. On each rod was a step, which at every shuttle stopped opposite a 'sollar', a small platform. Going up you stepped off the rod at the top of its lift, either onto the sollar to await the next rise, or with a double installation onto the rod alongside, at the bottom of its drop and about to lift again. This brought you quite quickly 'to grass.' The descent was from rod to rod or sollar in reverse.

Levant, like other mines which operated almost on the shore, drove its galleries under the sea. There were sections where the miners, working upwards along the face of a lode, could hear beyond the hammering of picks and drills boulders rolling along the seabed in storm time. Sometimes the 'tributers', the team of tinners working under contract, in their quest of the brown ore would drive too near the seabed and the sea would break through. An old miner who had been there when this happened in the 1870's told Dr. Hamilton Jenkin all about it. "I can mind the day the four men was drowned holing through into the house of water (i.e. the sea) in North Levant. 'Twas a Monday and I was working afternoon core out Spearn. They say the end they was driving had been bone-dry all along. When the men got down that day they stopped out at the beginning of the level to touch a pipe of bacca, and told the boy to go in and clear up the end 'gainst they started to work. Over a while the boy came out and said 'We ain't far off the water now, Uncle Nick, for 'tes running through in the end.' 'Git away,' said the man, 'thee'st took fear, booy.' What happened after that they don't know, but 'tis supposed the men went in to work and the first blow they struck on the drill, the water burst through upon them. One man was found afterwards with the tram (= the barrow for carrying the ore) thrown on top of him yards back in the level, and one they never found for a week. The two other men, as I said, I seed myself broft into the carpenters' shop and laid out 'pon the binch."

That was not the last disaster to befall the old Levant. This occurred on 20th October 1919, leaving widows and orphans and driving the mine out of existence. By then Cornish mines, or at any rate the survivors of forty years of 'knacked bals', of closures, had exchanged the outdated man-engine for the cage, which dropped you down so fast, so far, that it took a sickening second for your stomach to catch up with you. But not at the Levant, which had money problems. Yet hadn't they all, ever since cheap alluvial tin from Malaya crashed the commodity market? Plans were in hand at the Levant, though, and indeed one cage had been installed at the mine. Half a mile out under the sea a vertical shaft, aptly known as the New Submarine Shaft, had been sunk to an even deeper level. Here the cage operated. Do you not find it amazing that a lift should be in use not merely so deep in the bowels of the earth, but also fathoms under the seabed? It almost gives credence to the belief that a troglodyte civilisation flourishes beneath earth's surface!

It is three o'clock that fateful afternoon, almost a year after the Armistice, when the slaughter ceased on the Western Front. Their core over, the weary miners are rising 'to grass', mounted on every step of the creaking old man-engine. On, off, on, off, up, up, up, each man standing in his own little globe of candle light; a twinkling succession rising out of the darkness. Day is a glim at the mouth of the narrow shaft, visible to the men at the top, growing as they mount towards it; and already the air is freshening. Lift, lower, lift shuttles the engine - and a bearing breaks! The highest rod telescopes into the next, that into the rod beneath it, and so the whole way down. The men are crushed by the falling timber, tossed off into the shaft, and men and timber cry out and crash through utter dark onto the miners below.

Thirty-one were killed, twelve dreadfully injured. It was days before the bodies were all recovered. Seventy-five children were left fatherless. Eleven of these, brothers and sisters of one family, had just lost their mother too. A commemorative plaque was unveiled at Trewellard Methodist Church by the Lord Lieutenant - sixty-three years later. The sole surviving widow attended the service. She was ninety. As for the Levant mine, it limped on for another eight years or so and then expired.

CHAPTER NINE

THE LOST LAND

You must couple folk-lore with history to understand, though neither will quite explain, the mysteries of the Cornish moors - hill and headland forts and settlements, from which successive invaders drove the natives to settle in their turn; menhirs and cromlechs and circles of stones where, when the 'fluence is on you, you can almost glimpse priests and nameless kings stalking through the heather. On the West Way to St. Ives below Trencrom Hill, and duly attested by the National Trust, you will see one of the bowling stones of the giants there which rolled out of play during a game with Cormoran of the Mount. Cormoran, you will recall if you are so fortunate as to have absorbed fairy tales at your mother's knee before T.V. took over, was the ogre slain by Jack the Giant Killer, his sword inscribed thereafter, "This is the valiant Cornishman who slew the giant Cormoran." Here folk-lore helps out history; for would you not suppose that Jack was a bronze age pioneer who, better armed with the metal he had mined ('Cousin Jack' being the traditional term for a Cornish miner) and with the cunning of a superior culture, disposed of the local chieftain? Some simple, thick-thewed precursor of Cornish 'wrastling' this champion would be, run to earth in his hutments on that great pyramidical lump of pink-brown granite once called Careg-cowze-en-clowze, the grey rock in the wood; on St. Michael's Mount then girdled with forest where iron ships sail today.

Weathering has rounded the boulders and hollowed out seats for the giants in the rocky outcrops on the hills, and through aeons of sand and salt and grit in the wind has poised the loggan stones at point of balance. These rocking stones once attracted the Zennor and St. Levan witches like moths about a candle flame, and seem still to be steeped in a sort of magic. You come across weird notions which survive from the dark worship of Earth Mother before history began. Celtic crosses, ubiquitous in the far West, do not always obscure the potent fetiches they were carved to efface. Out there on the moors facts are hardly more real than the forgotten memories which reach out to you from the granite and the peaty turf.

There are historic memories besides, kindlier if no less mystical, which haunt remote churches that, with their low slate roofs and squat towers, are one with the land they grew out of; a patina of memories immortalising the dedication of medieval craftsmen and the generations who worshipped there.

While lovely things survive, the hand
That fashioned them, or fondled them, lives on
Adown what centuries soe'er
The dying footfall's gone.
Old churches ring
(Hark and you'll hear)
With chiselling,
And where forgotten folk would stand
To chant the creed, their fingers grip the pew
And leave the touch of love upon it too.

Perhaps a hundred and forty belfries will ring for you, even when they lie "full fathoms five" beneath Mounts Bay and offshore past Lands End; for folk will tell you in Penzance, tongue in cheek yet a little believing, that the bells of drowned churches toll there. You can hear them pealing yourself, or what the expectant mind interprets as such among the sea sounds, one being receptive in Cornwall to fancies that would get short shrift east of the River Tamar. These bells resurrect folk memories of an inundation that has been variously ascribed to oceanic calamities far, far away, and to centuries from before those of early man to that of the Norman conquest.

But there are facts you cannot ignore. A photograph of 1900 shows tree stumps uncovered in Mounts Bay at an exceptional ebb. The Victorian author Robert Hunt, a Fellow of the Royal Society, no less, observed "I have passed in a boat from St. Michael's Mount to Penzance on a summer day, when the waters were very clear and the tide low, and seen the black masses of trees in the white sands extending far out into the bay." But you do not have to go back a hundred years for evidence of the drowned woodland. Only a few years ago an abnormal tide and a wild wind laid the stumps bare again, so that you could walk among them and mourn the vanished boughs.

It is claimed that this sunken forest was part of the lost land of Lyonesse, medievally Loonois, Lethowsow in Old Cornish, from whose shores Sir Tristan fared forth to join, though some say to fight, King Arthur's knights at Tintagel, and got fatefully entangled with Iseult the Fair. The Seven Stones reef eighteen miles due west of Lands End, where the lightship is stationed and where the giant tanker 'Torrey Canyon' struck in '67, was known in Scilly as 'the Town.' Here we are told flourished the City of Lions, capital of Lyonesse. Fishermen once trawled-up the base of a stone column from the Seven Stones, three feet in diameter and half that high, besides fragments of glazed windows and other masonry, while beneath the surface they saw the tops of buildings. Or so it is said. Perhaps our latter-day mermen, aqua-lunged and wet-suited, when they have exhausted the surprises of Admiral Shovel's flagship

'Association' and her doomed consorts upon the Scilly shoals, and sorted out the remaining deep water treasure trove on the West Cornwall seabed, will render a verdict.

At Lands End, if you will turn your back upon the encroachments of Concrete Age Man there and look seaward, it is not difficult in calm weather to picture the parishes and pastures of the lost land, and the oak forests which then covered Cornwall too, stretching far below into the sunset. The Scillies are once more a mountain cluster beyond lowlands which, apart from a few heights, and the towering Lion City sprawling across the Seven Stones like Rome on her seven hills, rise scarcely higher above the tide than the ancient Pilgrims' Way from St. Erth to Marazion that almost makes Penwith an island today. It was to Scilly, fabled Celtic country of the dead whose tombs you may still explore - to Avalon, no matter what the Glastonbury Arthurians say! - that the mourning queens ferried great Arthur after the battle in the mist.

Robert Hunt F.R.S. knew a vicar of St. Erth whose female relative dreamed a dream, followed its prescription, prepared a potion, and with appropriate incantations poured it into the sea off Lands End. The object of the ritual was to resurrect Lyonesse from the deep, in every respect just as it had been. But, he quotes:

> "Perchance some form was unobserved,
> Perchance in prayer or faith she swerved."

For nothing happened.

The reverse process, the engulfing of the land, was envisaged by Rev. Whitfield, a romancer of the mid-1800's. He rounds off Malory's 'Morte d'Arthur' with Arthur's knights, their stricken king having been borne off to Avalon in his funereal barge, fleeing across Lyonesse before victorious Mordred and the rebel array. Merlin appears, conjured up somehow from the enchantress Nimue's cavern. At his command the earth quakes and Lyonesse sinks beneath the waves, traitors and all, leaving the loyal Round Tablers high and dry. One prefers the single-minded conviction of the other parson's female relative!

The ancient families of Trevelyan and Vyvyan, Cornish both, display in their armorial bearings the charger on which an ancestor outpaced the lapping surf. The inundation seems to have been steady rather than sudden, as if the flooding tide, having devoured the beach in its usual twice-daily spectacle, one day refused to disgorge but ate its way beyond the high water mark and on and on and on. The Trevelyans managed to evacuate their livestock as well as themselves, Trevelyan himself remaining until the last herdsman had clambered to higher ground at Perranuthnoe. A cave there used to be shown as the very spot where the knight dismounted, safe at last.

As for the Vyvyans, who have been West Cornwall landowners for over eight hundred years, probably a great deal over, Lady Clara explains that the white horse of their crest also commemorates the steed on which a forbear cheated the cataclysm. Vyvyan tradition maintains that for centuries a white horse, saddled like the "horse passant furnished proper" they sported on their helms, was kept stabled at Trelowarren, the family seat, against a recurrence of the emergency. It had been a shock which, as you can see, took a prodigious time to work out of their system, and besides emphasising how terrifying it must be to find the tide still at your heels however far you ride inland, gives substance to the belief that it really did happen. Regrettably nothing is known of the other Vyvyans, their dependents and cattle on that desperate occasion. We can but hope that they had scurried on ahead.

Records of a third escape shows how the inundation occurred on the north as well as on the south shores of the Lands End peninsula. There was a lord of Goonhilly (where Satellite Station Earth probes the heavens from the Lizard plateau) with estates in Lyonesse who built an oratory - Chapel Idne, the narrow chapel - at Sennen as a thank-offering for his deliverance.

Scoffers dismiss the Lost Land story as pure legend. You confuse it with the Atlantis myth, they say; with the civilisation superior to our own that flourished in mid-Atlantic, or was it in mid-Mediterranean? and was swallowed up by a rise in the sea level or dragged down by an earthquake, or blown out of existence by a volcanic explosion, or even lost control of its nuclear experiments. And if this cataclysm really did happen off Cornwall, they say, it must have occurred long before Man followed the bison trail from the Spanish grasslands. What if Florence, the Saxon monk of Worcester, did jot down in the Anglo-Saxon Chronicle that on 11th November, 1099, the region between Lands End and the Scillies disappeared "when the sea overflowed the shore, destroying towns and drowning many persons and innumerable oxen and sheep?" So William, also of Worcester, faithfully confirmed his predecessor's report four hundred years later! Little a cloistered Benedictine at the turn of the eleventh century knew of the world outside his convent wall, and less still that other recluse could have told about such remote and uncertain times! The aged Florence, the scoffers continue, would have heard of the great tide of 1099 when meadowland became the Goodwin Sands and, according to the Elizabethan historian Stow, "the sea brake over the banks of the Thames." Certainly if Lyonesse, hitherto a bulwark against the rage of ocean, had been overwhelmed so releasing a mighty surge into the Channel, the flooding of the late King Harold Godwinsson's easternmost domains, low lying as they were, was likely enough within the week.

Cornwall's native chronicler, Richard Carew, disappointingly makes no reference to Lyonesse. Out of sight, out of mind! However his

Land's End - from Cyrus Redding's Itinerary

contemporary, John Norden the map-maker, devotes an interesting paragraph or two to the cataclysm. "It is lefte vnto this age by tradition (the original rendering, Tudor spelling and all, is too charming to up-date) that a great parte of this Promontorie is swallowed vp of the deuowring sea, namelye, the Countrye of Lioness and other Lande somtime lying betwene the present Landes end and the Iles of Scillye 30 myles distant.

"......But the Sea, ayded by tyme and tempests, is euery where a powrefull adversarie to the Land, and in moste places the Lande weake to resiste: And therfore ther mighte be suche a Lioness parte of this promontorie deuored with the Sea, beying so fierclye besett on eyther syde with violent surges of the merciles Ocean.

"The place wher Lioness is supposed to haue lyen is now called of the inhabitantes and seafaring men Lethowsow...... at this day, it is obserued that the Sea muche preuayleth not: thowgh the wether-beaten mounte of St. Michaell stande nowe an vnmoueable rock: yet by the Etymon (etymology) of the britishe phrase it seemeth that the situation of this invincible rock is chaunged from Cara Cowze in clowze, the Browne rock in the wood, into the browne rock in the sea."

On most counts we may assume that the frontiers of Lyonesse included the Isles of Scilly and extended from Cape Cornwall right round to the Lizard: that when after one of our several ice ages water masses from melted icebergs broke through between Ushant and Scilly to make the English Channel, Lethowsow was spared for a high measure of civilisation and a catastrophe all the more direful for delay. Nevertheless the seekers of the Lost Land do not all agree that Lyonesse lay west of the Duchy of Cornwall. Some place it between Rame Head, on the Cornish side of Plymouth Sound, and the Dodman, south of Mevagissey, treetops having been sighted thereabouts two fathoms down. Here, Thomas the Rhymer chanted around 1170, once rose the proud city of Caerleon where Tristan of Lyonesse was born, albeit others hold that the hero's birthplace was in a wood on the way there. It was from Caerleon, they maintain, and not from the City of Lions, that Tristan was kidnapped by rovers as a young knight and launched on that complicated career of valour and love and deception extolled by troubadours, immortalised in the annals of chivalry.

Castle Dore in neighbouring Cornwall survives to this day, an Iron-Age fort within whose grass-grown, unpretentious ramparts you will find a medieval palace, or what little is left of it, looking towards the present Carlyon Bay. King Mark of Cornwall held court there. And from Castle Dore the wayward lovers Tristan and Iseult, he the nephew and she the queen of the deceived monarch, journeyed together in easy stages and mutual enchantment by way of Grampound and Malpas, down-river from Truro, to meet royal Arthur; perhaps also to teach Queen Guenivere a thing or two about pulling the wool over the eyes of kings.

The Dodman-Lizard span too has claims on Lyonesse. The Black

Rock which yachtsmen swish past dead centre in the Fal estuary, a 7-foot finger of rock at low tide topped by a beacon, was once recorded as a large island at high water though otherwise joined to the shore. This was not only the vanished kingdom, or part at least thereof, but "was in Old Time the Island (viz. the Ikta) of Diodorus Siculus, by which Tin was transported into Gallia." A conclusion, from which most would differ, that much reduces the standing of St. Michael's Mount in the history of early Cornwall.

Where then lay the Lost Land - if Lost Land there ever was? Westward or south'ard? Both or neither? There is so much to resolve, and the savants will have to work on it, carbon dating and all - which you can be pretty certain won't come about until, and then only as a bonus, they have satisfied their quest for oil in the Western Approaches and turned their minds instead to feeding our great-grandchildren from the offshore gardens of the sea.

Meanwhile you can only wonder and trust that feeling in your bones, as you cruise towards the islands in the 'Scillonian', or stare down from the helicopter once its shadow has slipped from green fields into the diffusing grey of the waves, that down below you people lived out their little lives until doomsday came in a roar of waters. Recollections of a Britain land-linked to Europe, as it certainly was once, may indeed be fossilized in folk memory: Man has inhabited Earth a mighty long time. But later memories have been preserved, however imperfectly. Trevelyan and Vyvyan traditions, legend, monkish gossip of long ago give more than a hint that Lyonesse stretched away from Lands End into the sunset; that Cornishmen, or their kinfolk, tilled and built, hunted, loved, worshipped and fought there.

What further proof should we incorrigible romantics ask? We recall, as if the experience were our own, the refugees pressing towards the cliff wall of the Penwith highlands, scrambling up to a new life in Cornwall. We watch the knights spurring ahead of the reaching tide with better luck than Pharaoh's warriors had in the Red Sea. The flood swells across the plain. The belfries tolling the tocsin fall silent one by one. The sea level rises to drown even the roof tops of the Lion City, there on the Seven Stones of Lethowsow, until the peaks of Avalon loom alone on the Atlantic horizon.

LYONESSE

There's froth on the snaffle, blood on the spurs,
The surf's at our hooves as we lengthen the stride,
The waves lap the ploughland and smother the furze,
The blush of the heather has blanched in the tide.

I've opened the fold, unlatched stable and byre,
Freed my proud hawks from hood, bewit and jess,
Harnessed sleek Hermes, stout hunter, fast flier,
And heath, field and forest we flee Lyonesse.

The flood's on the lowlands, eddying, surging,
Woods are awash, the creek villages drowned,
Peasants and beasts on the hill-forts converging
Watch, wailing and lowing, the waters close round.

Lion City behind me, seven-hilled Lethowso'
Swarms like a hive at the tocsin's brisk peal;
East - Channel's rising! Rein north hard by Mowso'
Cold sweat in the saddle, hot panic at heel.

Sir Vyvyan overtakes, grey charger bolting,
Trevelyan jogs, herding his cattle. Then with
Riders and walkers and ox-waggons jolting
We cross Marghadyou for the wastes of Penwith.

Lyonesse, Lyonesse, soft you lived, hard you died!
Blest Avalon's summits alone breathe the air,
Merfolk through your green, haunted silences glide,
Adrift with the wrack things unspeakable stare.

Three landless gaze west, mute in grief, at St. Levan,
Strangers - Trevelyan, young Vyvyan and I -
Sick for home; better with those home in heaven
We, passing, saw praying and kissing goodbye!

But most of our comrades Atlantic took cursing
Old Bouca, the sea-god, they'd called in distress.
No pity! No sparing! Isles, flotsam dispersing
Are all of the Kingdom we loved, Lyonesse.

Remember in Kernow, you all the years after
Whose keels skim Lethowso' as home your ships press,
This land of the oak wood, its loving and laughter,
And oceans colliding across Lyonesse.

ST. IVES HERITAGE

by Lena and Donald Bray, Cornish Publications.

"This is a patient, well-researched and loving look at the history, customs and general lifestyle of this jewel of the North Cornish coast, enlivened by many personal reminiscences that make this an unusually endearing narrative. ...... St. Ives history....... told delightfully."

(Western Morning News)

"...... a book that will be enjoyed by many...... it is a story which spans the years, the people, and the events and industries, told in an affectionate and personal way."

(The Cornishman)

"...... a remarkable book it is: a real labour of love, as rich and Cornish as Figgy Pudden...... The story of St. Ives is told with great relish."

(Cornish Life)

"...... is being read by Cornish families all over the world."

(St. Ives Times & Echo)

"It is a delightful book, and I congratulate you on the whole achievement."

(Professor W.G. Hoskins)

Relevant Books &c consulted, read with pleasure, dipped into over many years:-

FOOTPRINTS IN FAR CORNWALL ... ... R.S. Hawker
CORNISH CHARACTERS & STRANGE EVENTS ... S. Baring Gould
HISTORY OF CORNWALL ... ... F.E. Halliday
MEDIEVAL CORNWALL ... ... Elliot Binns
PAROCHIAL HISTORY OF CORNWALL (ed. Lake) ... ... R. Polsue
SURVEY OF CORNWALL ... ... Richard Carew
DESCRIPTION OF CORNWALL ... ... John Norden
ILLUSTRATED ITINERARY OF THE COUNTY OF CORNWALL ... ... Cyrus Redding
EXCURSIONS IN THE COUNTY OF CORNWALL ... F.W.L. Stockdale
PARLIAMENTARY REPRESENTATION IN CORNWALL ... ... W.T. Lawrance
CORNWALL IN THE AGE OF THE INDUSTRIAL REVOLUTION ... ... J. Rowe
CORNWALL, HISTORY OF THE LANDSCAPE ... ... W.G.V. Balchin
THE CORNISH MINER ... ... A.K. Hamilton Jenkin
CORNWALL & ITS PEOPLE ... ... A.K. Hamilton Jenkin
CORNISH SHIPWRECKS ... ... Clive Carter
WRECK & RESCUE ROUND THE CORNISH COAST C. Noall & G. Farr
TALES OF THE CORNISH SMUGGLERS ... ... John Vivian
CORNWALL ... ... John Betjeman
CORNWALL & THE ISLES OF SCILLY ... ... (ed. Sean Jennett)
POPULAR ROMANCES OF THE WEST OF ENGLAND ... ... R. Hunt
HEARTHSIDE STORIES ... ... W. Bottrell
RAMBLES BEYOND RAILWAYS ... ... Wilkie Collins
STORY OF CORNWALL'S RAILWAYS ... ... A. Fairclough
TUDOR CORNWALL ... ... A.L. Rowse
KINGDOM OF DUMNONIA ... ... Susan Pearce
PADSTOW ... ... Claude Berry
GWITHIAN ... ... Charles Thomas
HISTORY OF HAYLE ... ... Virginia Bliss
HARVEYS OF HAYLE ... ... E. Vale
OLD NEWQUAY ... ... S.T. Husband
HAYLE ... ... A.G. Digues La Touche
OLD MINES OF PHILLACK & GWITHIAN ... A.G. Digues La Touche
EARLY HISTORY OF HAYLE FOUNDRY ... ... Stephen Michell
MINING IN PHILLACK & GWITHIAN ... ... J. Hambley Rowe
ISTHMUS OF PENWITH ... ... Ivor Thomas
HISTORY OF ST. IVES, LELANT, TOWEDNACK & ZENNOR ... ... J.H. Matthews
JOURNAL (unpublished) ... ... W.J. Jacobs
ENCYCLOPAEDIA BRITANNICA

CORNISH MAGAZINE Vol. I
CORNISH LIFE MAGAZINE
ROYAL CORNWALL GAZETTE
WESTERN ECHO
ST. IVES TIMES & ECHO
CORNISHMAN
WEST BRITON

The author regrets inevitable omissions.

CORNISH PUBLICATIONS

Published by Dyllansow Truran -
Truran Publications, Trewolsta, Trewirgie, Redruth 216796

LITERATURE AND POETRY

CORNISH BEDSIDE BOOK No. 1. - by John Keast 9506431 8 1

Place-Names, customs, dialects, remedies and recipes are nicely balanced by short essays and stories by early travellers, historical events and extracts from diaries. A thoroughly entertaining book.

Card Covers - £1.65

VISITORS TO CORNWALL - by Ida Procter 0 907566 27 8 P/B
0 907566 26 X H/B

As J.C. Trewin says in his Introduction - "Ida Procter can recreate her guests most surely... Everyone is here; Francis Kilvert for example, Celia Fiennes is here - At St. Austell. Nearly two centuries later the young Beatrix Potter was arriving by train at Falmouth.
It is an enchanting book."

Paperback £3.50
Hardback £5.95

HOW LONG IS FOREVER - Memories of a Cornish Maid 0 907566 30 8 C/C
- by Ethelwyn Watts 0 907566 89 8 H/B

Born it the changing years of the decade that followed the First World War, the author describes her home parish as "perhaps the most Cornish part of Cornwall" and she paints a word picture of a magical land.

Card Covers £1.85
Hard Back £3.95

THE BOUNCING HILLS - Dialect Tales and Light Verse 0 907566 38 3 C/C
by Jack Clemo 0 907566 39 1 H/C

Jack Clemo says "I contributed many dialect tales to Cornish Almanacks before the war capturing the lighter side of Clay country village life as it was 50 years ago. I have chosen eight of these stories, and have added a selection of my comic verse (not in dialect, but with a Cornish flavour.) There are about 20 short poems, mostly written for or about children.
This is a book from a Cornish literary giant shedding a new light on Cornwall's own blind poet.

Card covers £3.65
Hard Covers £6.75

THE HISTORY OF FALMOUTH - by Dr. James Whetter 0 907566 01 4 H/B
0 907566 02 2 C/C

The author's considerable knowledge of life in the 17th Century Cornwall provides much new information about the origins of the old town - its growth over about three and a half centuries and its social, cultural and religious history.

Hard Covers £4.95
Card Covers £2.95

CARN BREA - by Michael Tangye 0 907566 11 1 C/C

A book on Redruth, Illogan and Camborne's dominating feature. Micael Tangye's expert account will meet the needs of students of all ages and all of those who are curious about 'the Carn'. Illustrated by the author.

Card covers £1.95

CORNISH EPITAPHS Vol. 1. - by John Keast 0 907566 15 4

Records, humour, pathos AND sermons in stone! Beautifully illustrated with photographs, line-drawings, etc. This is Volume one of a two-volume work.

Card Covers £1.65

THE LIFE OF PASSMORE EDWARDS - R.S. Best 0 907566 23 5 H/C
(With an essay on the life of Sylvanus Trevail 0 907566 18 9 C/C
by Peter Laws)

Rising from rags to ri ches, he endowed nearly 70 institutions -libraries, art galleries, hospitals, museums and an orphanage etc. throughout Britain between the years of 1890 and 1904. The first substantial biography of the great Cornish Benefactor.

Hard Covers £3.95
Card Covers £~~1.95~~

THE SAINTS OF CORNWALL - by Catherine Rachel John 0 907566 14 6 L/C
0 907566 13 8 H/C

A comprehensive account of the many saints of Cornwall - dedications ranging from early Celtic to modern times. Miss John has built on the researches of her father, (Donald Attwater) Canon Doble, and others. Illustrated with 40 photos and line-drawings.

Linen Covers £7.80
Hard Covers £11.95

MEMORIES OF OLD PENRYN - by the late Florence Rapson 0 907566 42 1
Edited by Rita Tregellas Pope

A picture of a way of life of which only nostalgic memories remain.

£1.85

ST. IVES HERITAGE - By Lena & Donald Bray 0 907566 07 3 H/B
0 907566 08 1 C/C

Recollections and records of St. Ives, Carbis Bay and Lelant. "This patient, well researched and loving look at the history, customs and general lifestyle of this jewel of the North Cornish Coast makes this an unusually endearing narrative" Western Morning News.

Hard Covers £4.95
Card Covers £2.95

JOHN KNILL - HIS LIFE AND TIMES - by Beryl James 0 907566 06 5

"John Knill, Mayor of St. Ives, customs official and adventurer extraordinary, was a remarkable son of the rumbustious 18th century... The life-style of this lawyer-cum-pursuer of smugglers makes a scenario fit for any Hollywood epic.

Card Covers £1.50

CORNISH SAYINGS AND REMEDIES 0 907566 04 9
by Kathleen Hawke.

What makes all Mrs. Hawke's work on dialect particularly interesting is that she has lived for many years in both mid-Cornwall and west-Cornwall". K.C. Philips.

90p

CORNISH QUIZ - by R.S. Best 9506431 4 9

Over 500 questions and answers on Cornwall and things Cornish. Illustrated by C.M. Pellowe.

95p

MEMORIES OF A TRURONIAN IN WAR AND PEACE - - by Rex Barratt 0 907566 00 6

The picture of the city that emerges, how it adapted its ways of life to war, the excitement of Royal Visits, life in church and school, politics, music and drama, shopkeepers and local characters, are all faithfully recorded and illustrated.

Card Covers £1.30

MUSIC

THE CAROLS OF THOMAS MERRITT 9506431 7 3

The best-loved carols of the Illogan composer. A thousand monuments of the last great mining generation are now destroyed or decaying, but the notes jof Thomas Merritt's music, rising to a new climax each Christmas, continue to enshrine the ancient Christian and Celtic spirit of Cornwall.

Card Covers 85p

CAROLS OF CORNWALL - arranged by Kenneth Pelmear 0 907566 22 7

With a historic review of the development of the Christmas Carol in Cornwall to the time of Thomas Merritt.

Card Covers £1.20

CORNISH VOICES 0 907566 21 9

Ten hymns and anthems arranged by Kenneth Pelmear, all popular with Cornish choirs and including "Hail to The Homeland" (Hayl dh'agan Mamvro!!) and "A Celtic Benediction".

Card Covers 85p

CANOW KERNOW 0 907566 25 1

The long-awaited reprint of this fine volume of traditional Cornish folk-songs, edited by Inglis Gundry and revised to include two additional songs from the Hutchens manuscript.

Laminated Card £2.40

SLAUTE TO TRURO - Commemorative Music - by Kenneth Pelmear 0 907566 31 6

Composed to mark the Centenary of the City of Truro and to similarly honour the Centenary of Truro School. (Voices and Organ copy).

Card Covers £1.35

A ST. PIRAN MISCELLANY - Kemysk Sen Perran - by Brian Webb 0 907566 44 8

The stories and traditions of Cornwall's Patron Saint. Told in Cornish and in English.

75p

JOWAN CHY AN HORTH - Examined -by Gwas Kenethlow (John Page) 0 907566 36 7

300 years ago Nicholas Boson wrot to Jowan Chy an Horth to teach his children Cornish, and today, 300 years later, it can scarcely be improved upon as an aid to teaching.

Card Cover £1.20

NEBES WHETHLOW BER - Caradar (A.S.D. Smith) 0 907566 10 3

A long awaited reprint of eleven of Caradar's short stories.

75p